# Beats and Elements

# Beats and Elements: A Hip Hop Theatre Trilogy

### Katie Beswick and Conrad Murray

**No Milk for the Foxes** *Paul Cree and Conrad Murray*
**DenMarked** *Conrad Murray*
**High Rise eState of Mind** *David Bonnick Jr, Paul Cree, Lakeisha Lynch-Stevens and Conrad Murray*

*With a foreword by*
JONZI D

*methuen* | drama
LONDON · NEW YORK · OXFORD · NEW DELHI · SYDNEY

METHUEN DRAMA
Bloomsbury Publishing Plc
50 Bedford Square, London, WC1B 3DP, UK
1385 Broadway, New York, NY 10018, USA
29 Earlsfort Terrace, Dublin 2, Ireland

BLOOMSBURY, METHUEN DRAMA and the Methuen Drama logo are trademarks of
Bloomsbury Publishing Plc

First published in Great Britain 2022

# Contents

# Shout Outs

True to hip hop, have to give shout outs, big ups, props to these people for inspiring and helping in many different ways:

Barry Murray, Gavin Salim, Chucko, Peter Green, Tyrone Rhoomes, Monique Duchen, Jeanne Le Cocq and Peter Seddon.

Trish Reid – you always encouraged us with our hip hop theatre ideas from TdC til now. It meant a lot then, and still means a lot. Big up KU crew.

Lara Taylor – producer of *No Milk,* championed *High Rise* and a whole lot more. You are actually one of the realest.

Lizzy Raskit – you championed TdC and brought me along to do what we have done with the BAC Beatbox Academy. Thanks for everything and for being the producer of *DenMarked* and a lot of other of my projects.

Sarah Q – you told me to make *DenMarked* a thing, and told me to fix up. Thank you.

Warren Fitzgerald – thanks bro. Hope we can connect again.

Richard Dufty for your feedback (and enthusiasm for *DenMarked*).

Harun Morrisson, Andrea Brooks (thanks for calling me a \*\*\*\*, it helped), Toma Dim, Rosie (thanks for that lift to the station at Latitude, thought I was gonna die), Bethany Haynes and Matt Peover.

Camden People's Theatre – thanks for letting Beats & Elements do what we do. Brian, Kaya, James and DANIEL! (Dan – we miss you), Malachy Orozco and Anna O' Dell.

Simeon Miller – thanks for your amazing lighting design skills. When we doing it again?

My *DenMarked* touring crew: Maverick (delete that video from Peterborough!), free3flow (outta space bro), Nahum – day one academy member! Big up bro, J unique – I'll never forget them mad clubs, Kate – you touched down once, but Wigan was sick!

Lyrici – you guys! I love you.

GL4 – I class you as family – you inspire me – thank you! (Hold tight Elfy).

Strike A Light – you are 100 real and part of our journey! Thank you. Let's do more.

Jumped Up Theatre.

David Jubb – triple OG – thank you.

Mc Mello – thanks for the history lessons, lenzez (greatest grime spitter in the UK), Fezzy aka Fez One, pick n mix, Dolli, Ange, Greg Hall, crazy cayne, Tubby Boy, Carl Chamberlin, prime time, Scottee, BBC London, London Live, Barbican Lab, Darren Randen and Well Versed Ink, Reena, Jumped Up Festival, Sandra Quartey, Derby Theatre, Brighton Dome, Folkestone Quarterhouse, Surma Centre, Sam Lithgo, UK UNSIGNED, John Downie, Mariam, Alex Mermikides, Charley Genever, David Graham, South Thames College, Katie Taborn and Becky Hall.

Marcia Oliver – thanks for believing in me as an actor/singer/director. Many artists and performers passed through your doors and added to the UK performing arts scene.

YPT/Homegrown/BBA crew members, participants and artists. You tried out many of the ideas and practices that made these plays, so thank you.

Shout outs to Roland for the discount on my RC 505.

My social worker Julie Morro. Thank you. You listened. And you were SO tall ... or maybe I was just really small?

– Love, Conrad.

# Foreword

## Why hip hop theatre?

*Born and bred in Bow. Near the flyover*
*Sleeping on a sofa, never seen a chauffeur*
*Money was tight, man. Even for the white man*
*The bluefoot crew took the piss in their white vans*
*Every other day, where the brothers stay, undercover say*
*'Nigger boy!' You're inside for another day*
*And the quest for sess was stress*
*Wishing for the DHL effect, for my DHSS cheque . . .*

I wrote that rhyme in 1991. I had never seen a chauffeur. But to be fair, the sofa line was pure ghetto embellishment. I slept in a nice single bed in a tiny, untidy bedroom. The spoilt last child.

Everything else was the truth though. Everyone was brock pocket in the 70s. Black, white, Asian. Don't matter how many sovereigns you had on your fingers, or how much you paid for your sheepskin, we were the east London working class. And we were proud.

The police have always, ALWAYS been dickheads. Not just because of the shape of their helmets. They would constantly harass us while we hung out on the streets of Bow. A posse of mostly Black boys always draws suspicion from racists, especially those protected by a racist institution. I've been arrested three times, and not one led to a conviction.

So, practicing contemporary dance in this climate was interesting. My secondary school never had drama on the curriculum, which had always been my first love since primary school. But dance was a great option. I never had any issues with the man dem as a man child choosing dance. Fortunately, one of the hardest boys in my year chose dance as an option, so I was fearless in fearsome company. For my end of year performance, I borrowed my friend's cosh to create a Martha Graham influenced dance about gang violence. I was wearing torn lycra while performing, not sure if my costume idea was the right one. My dance teacher reported me to the headmaster for carrying a 'deadly' weapon. I still passed my exam with flying coloured coshes.

Rap music was revealed to me by my older brothers. 'Rapper's Delight' by The Sugarhill Gang was phenomenal to me. The fast, rhythmic chatter reminded me of reggae toasting, but with an American accent. I learned as many of the lyrics as I could, and realised I made everyone happy when I recited them. My first hip hop props. It felt good. I was ten years old.

Graffiti and breaking were next. When I first saw an early documentary about hip hop I couldn't believe the physical dexterity of the Rocksteady Crew. So many 'How they do that??' moments that everyone tried it the next day in school. All over the country. Including me. I loved breaking, I wasn't the best, but I tried until I realised emceeing was a better fit.

Interestingly, the idea of bringing these elements together never occurred to me. If anything, I wanted to keep contemporary dance and my love of hip hop completely separate. My emceeing was becoming 'a thing', and I didn't want ANYONE to know that during daylight hours I was masquerading as a poncey, tight-wearing, ballet dancer. But if they wanted to use that against me in a battle, I was ready. . .

*I'll take you out 2 by tutu, sink you like a fondue, without my barres you'll have nothing to hold onto*

My disillusionment with hip hop began with the whole gangsta rap movement. I was never convinced with the type of lyrics that glorified 'killing niggas'. I always found it self-genocidal, exaggerated, and I maintain that it was by design. All pirate radio was banned, and the playlist meant that commercial DJs had to play a balanced amount of bullshit. Before that switch, artists like Public Enemy and KRS-One were instilling a revolutionary spirit in hip hop culture that was a threat to the status quo. The image of the Black man as a hero was replaced with the image of the Black man as a thug.

My disillusionment with contemporary dance was more about the middle-class, white environment. While training at the London School of Contemporary Dance I felt compromised a lot. Having to deal with the unconscious bias, the micro-aggressions and the fact that I was in the minority. My value system was very different to theirs. My music was different to theirs. My fashion, my eating habits, my political stance. It was exhausting.

So in 1995, I premiered *Lyrikal Fearta* in the Oval House Theatre. A performance made up of short solos and duets exploring hip hop disciplines. Featuring DJ Pogo scratching as soundscape. Rap as script. Breaking and popping as storytelling devices. 'Safe' uses popping and waving to introduce four monologues exploring self-control. 'Guilty' is a duet with B-boy Banxy playing a violent cop. 'Shoota' is a duet with a gun. 'Aeroplane Man' is a solo about a Black man from Bow travelling the world to find his true home. Very much cathartic content!

I called it 'Hip Hop Theatre' because I needed to promote it to the hip hop community. I thought that title would separate the real heads from the chaff. I knew that the content would fully relate to that audience, even if some of the ideas were a bit contemporary crazy. I was able to pull all my

influences together as one moment – in some way freeing me of the need
to choose. I can do both. I can do it all.

So can you.

– Jonzi D

\*

**Jonzi D** has been actively involved in British hip hop culture, rapping and
B-boying in clubs and on the street since the early 1980s. Since graduating
from London Contemporary Dance School, Jonzi has been committed to
the development of Hip Hop Theatre – a form which he is widely credited
as inventing. He was an Associate Artist with The Place and has performed
and created dance theatre pieces worldwide. He is an Associate Artist of
Sadler's Wells and is based at the theatre. Jonzi is the curator and host of
the acclaimed Breakin' Convention, the international hip hop dance theatre
festival, nominated for a South Bank Show award and now in its eighteenth
year.

# Author Biographies

**Katie Beswick** is an award-winning writer and academic. She currently works as a Senior Lecturer in Drama at the University of Exeter. In her academic work she is especially interested in the relationship between class, culture and city spaces – particularly housing. Her book *Social Housing in Performance: The English Council Estate on and off Stage* (Bloomsbury Methuen 2019) explores the representation of council estates in news media, film, television, music video and theatre. She has published widely in books and journals, and is a regular contributor to the music and culture magazine *Loud and Quiet*. With Conrad Murray she is the author of *Making Hip Hop Theatre: Beatbox and Elements* (Bloomsbury Methuen 2022).

**David Bonnick Jr** is a passionate and creative south London actor who, after starting his career at the age of sixteen, went on to study Acting at Mountview Academy of Theatre Arts. His screen roles include Bobby Brown in *Whitney and Bobby: Addicted to Love* for ITV, and a returning estate agent in *EastEnders* for BBC. On stage his work has been varied, working long term with the Young People's Theatre at the Battersea Arts Centre (BAC), performing elsewhere in shows including *The Day the Waters Came* and *Scratched* Out, and collaborating as a member of the theatre companies Theatre de Cunt and Beats & Elements. Jr is also a talented rap artist, who performs under the name Gambit Ace at music festivals such as Boomtown, Wilderness and I Luv Live. He has his own music available to stream and download.

**Paul Cree** is a poet, rapper, storyteller and co-founder of hip-hop theatre company Beats & Elements. He has performed around the UK at a variety of festivals and events such as Bestival, Latitude and The Edinburgh Fringe. His work has featured on BBC 1Xtra and BBC London. He has written and performed two solo shows: *A Tale From The Bedsit* (2013) and *The C/D Borderline* (2016) and is currently developing a solo work titled *Make Your Own Bed and Hope for the Best* (2021). He has also co-written and performed in the critically acclaimed Beats & Elements shows, *No Milk for the Foxes* (2015) and *High Rise eState of Mind* (2019). In 2018 he published his debut collection of poems and stories, entitled *The Suburban*, with Burning Eye Books.

**Lakeisha Lynch-Stevens** is an actor, writer, theatre-maker and an associate artist of Beats & Elements, who has performed and created for many theatres, platforms and locations UK-wide. She is hugely inspired by the crossed wires between theatre making and music and by finding the most unique ways to illuminate complex stories. Lakeisha directs both Camden Youth Theatre and Uncover Theatre and was a Jenny Harris Award nominee in 2015. Credits include *High Rise eState of Mind* (Beats & Elements), *The Fellowship Project* (The Working Party), *Cards for Tyrone* and *Birthday Wish* (British Urban Film Festival).

**Conrad Murray** is a multi award-winning theatre maker, writer, director, rapper, beatboxer, live looper and singer. Based in Mitcham, south west London, he is passionate about making hip hop and beatbox theatre. He uses his Anglo-Indian working-class background to address issues such as class, race and heritage. He was listed as one of the Top 100 in *The Stage* newspaper's annual industry list in 2021, and was named in *The Observer*'s top ten theatre shows of the year in 2020 for his work as musical director and composer on Pilot Theatre's *Crongton Knights*. Since 2003, Conrad has been pioneering new modes of theatre, experimenting with hip hop forms, and has performed across the UK and internationally. He is Artistic Director of the BAC Beatbox Academy and a founder member of the theatre company Beats & Elements.

# This Collection

*Beats and Elements* is an anthology collection that brings together three hip hop performance texts authored by theatre maker Conrad Murray – one solo show and two plays co-written with a mix of collaborators from the Beats & Elements theatre company (David Bonnick Jr, Paul Cree and Lakeisha Lynch-Stevens). The collection also includes essay reflections on the works and an interview with the Beats & Elements company, written and compiled by Katie Beswick, the anthology editor, who has also collaborated with Murray on the book *Making Hip Hop Theatre: Beatbox & Elements* (Bloomsbury Methuen 2022), for which this anthology serves as a sister-text.

Murray's work has been much-acclaimed by critics and practitioners working in the UK theatre industry in recent years. *Frankenstein: How to Make a Monster* (2018) was the breakout show from the BAC Beatbox Academy, the community music-theatre programme for which Murray serves as Artistic Director. The show used beatbox techniques to craft a retelling of Mary Shelley's most famous novel. After almost two decades innovating with elements of hip hop (particularly rap and beatbox) and theatre ensemble collaboration, *Frankenstein* attracted mainstream attention for Murray, who co-directed the piece, and the Academy, garnering glowing five star reviews, coverage in major national newspapers, a run in Adelaide, Australia, and numerous awards.[1] It was adapted for television by the BBC, and at the time of writing plans to tour the world following the Covid-19 pandemic are in place. However, although *Frankenstein* showcases the collaborative, ensemble and community methods Murray has pioneered with the Beatbox Academy, it doesn't quite explicitly capture the specific social context which has driven much of Murray's work both within and outside the Academy, and the political consciousness that continues to underpin his ongoing practice.

The three plays included in this anthology, *No Milk for the Foxes*, *DenMarked* and *High Rise eState of Mind*, use hip hop to highlight the inequities produced by the UK's class system. They weave lyricism, musicality and dialogue to offer accounts of inner-city life written by working-class Londoners. This commitment to representing the working-class experience within specific political conditions and to platforming the stories of working-class people has fueled Murray's practice from his earliest collaborations with Theatre de Cunt (TdC) – the company he established with his brother, Barry 'Boston' Murray, in 2003 (although never officially disbanded, TdC ceased making theatre in 2010). The plays in this collection were developed between 2013 and 2019, following the establishment of a new company, Beats & Elements (with Paul Cree), and showcase an artist who has matured his practice, found a distinctive voice and process, and who has used this process to develop work with other artists too. The two introductory essays delve deeper into the background for the works that follow, thinking about the wider cultural, political and literary significance of the plays. The first essay gives a specific social and historical context that will help readers make sense of each of the plays, the second positions hip hop as a contemporary literary form and offers some ways to read hip hop texts as literature.

In this way, this collection positions Murray as a notable voice in the theatre arts. But importantly, although this volume celebrates and showcases Murray as an influential figure in contemporary performance, the collection emphasises collaboration and illustrates how other people have been instrumental throughout Murray's career, and in developing the works he has been involved with. The collaborative working method is explored in the interview with Beats & Elements members which follows the performance texts. The works published here all exist as a result of ensemble and collaborative working in one way or another, and, despite being framed around a named artist, this anthology eschews the concept of a 'star' or 'genius'. In other words, although this anthology is organised around the work of a single practitioner, the plays and supplementary material make explicit that theatre is always a collaborative process, and that excellence is always the result of talented, unique individuals working together to create a thing greater than the sum of each separate contribution.

## Note

1   For further reflections on *Frankenstein* see Maddy Costa, 'Beatbox
    Frankenstein: A reflection and interview with Conrad Murray', in Backpages
    of *Contemporary Theatre Review*, 29:4, pp. 493–5 (2019); and Maggie
    Inchley, '"It's Alive": Towards and Monsterized Theatre with Beatbox
    Academy's *Frankenstein: How to Make a Monster'*, *Contemporary Theatre
    Review*, 31:3, pp.307–22 (2021).

# Beats & Elements: Class and Hip Hop Theatre

In 2013, motivated by the journalist Owen Jones' book, *Chavs: The Demonisation of the Working Class*,[1] Conrad Murray and Paul Cree, performers, writers and theatre makers who had met at the Battersea Arts Centre (BAC) in south London, formed the theatre company Beats & Elements. Both were steeped in hip hop culture, and Murray had already gained experience applying hip hop techniques to theatre practice, both with his first company TdC, and with the BAC Beatbox Academy. The remit of Beats & Elements was to use original beats and instrumentals, along with selected elements of hip hop[2] – such as rapping, beatbox and style – to create theatre productions where working-class artists explore issues affecting working-class people.

As Jones' book points out, and as numerous sociologists and cultural studies scholars have noted,[3] the working classes have long been subject to stigmatising and degrading representations in popular culture. On screen and in newspapers, working-class people, or those perceived as working class, are often portrayed as criminals, as workshy benefit scroungers and as 'lacking' in social graces, intelligence and cultural knowledge. Perhaps the most egregious examples of this are in reality television shows, where working-class stories and lives are regularly exploited for entertainment.[4] During the 1990s, and into the 2000s and 2010s, tabloid television talk-shows such as *The Jerry Springer Show* in the USA and *Trisha* and *The Jeremy Kyle Show* in the UK, served up a regular menu of working-class dysfunction, exploiting 'ordinary' people navigating extremely difficult personal circumstances for entertainment. On *The Jeremy Kyle Show*, for example, guests who had experienced infidelity, were embroiled in family feuds or who had fallen out with close friends, were frequently subjected to polygraph and DNA tests, with the results broadcast on air. This exposure of highly personal situations, supported by unverified and often scientifically questionable 'proof', saw working-class people portrayed in the most unflattering light. Highly distressed guests were often dressed in cheap, ill-fitting clothing, with no or minimal make-up under stage-lighting, emphasising their most unattractive physical features. Because *Jeremy Kyle* was broadcast on ITV (one of the UK's most watched free-to-air broadcasters) most every weekday morning for seventeen seasons over fourteen years, the portrayals on the programme came to symbolise something about the working class in general, and to suggest through repetition that ugliness, lack of style and dysfunction served to characterise this group.[5] Reality documentaries (such as the much-criticised (*Benefits Street* Channel 4 2014), ubiquitous throughout the period, delivered similar narratives, and used the notion of 'reality' to conceal the fact that these were not 'real' portrayals of working-class lives in any meaningful sense, but highly mediated, edited and partial representations, almost always controlled by people who did not have lived experience of working-class culture. These supposedly 'real' portrayals are repeated in fictional cultural forms such as theatre, film and television, where working-class stories are again often told by or subject to the control of middle-class gatekeepers, and where ideas rooted in popular cultural forms such as reality television reinforce the veracity of the fiction. As Murray and I have discussed elsewhere, such portrayals almost always feel 'fake' to working-class people, despite being grounded in so-called reality.[6] In this way, cultural forms create stereotypes, which are projected onto those who are, or who are presumed to be, working class. Beats & Elements sought to counter such reductive representations, using the truths of the performers' own lives and experiences as a basis for story-telling.

Before we move on to consider the company's work in more detail, I make a brief diversion here, because to speak of 'working-class culture' is always to beg the question 'what (or who) is working class?' This question of definitions is frequently raised in conversations about class, and is important in many ways to enhancing our understanding of inequality. This is not least because, in order to understand and address inequality, we must have methods of measuring the factors that produce disadvantage. However, insisting on clear-cut definitions and requiring quantifiable measurements in order to make definitive statements about what class is and who can be perceived as legitimately working class is also a way that class injustice is sustained – refuting the existence of class by suggesting particular material conditions mean 'we are all middle class now'[7] has long been a tactic of the neoliberal governance which has, at the same time as effacing the existence of class hierarchies, paradoxically exacerbated class inequality. Issues of class are complex and, as the sociologist Pierre Bourdieu's widely cited work has indicated,[8] class inequities exist across a range of fields and capital is not only economic, but also social and cultural. All this is to say that, perhaps in the UK especially, class cannot be reduced to any simple definition. Your class identity is a relational as well as a fixed position, based on a range of intersecting experiences and feelings (both positive, negative and neutral), as well as the perceptions and projections of other people. In other words, what you think your class position is might not be what others perceive it to be. This matters because class inequality is also structured in part by how we treat one another to produce feelings of shame and pride, belonging and not belonging.[9] In Britain (and perhaps especially in England), class relations are produced within a context where a society once highly stratified around a rigid social system structured by heredity, ethnicity and occupation has become increasingly complex. This is due to a range of factors including but not limited to: increased social mobility in the latter half of the twentieth century due to the successes of the welfare state (and its later retraction due to the scaling back of welfare benefits under policies of neoliberalism and austerity); growing and systemic unemployment in particular regions due to the decline in industries such as coal mining and textile manufacturing; patterns of migration/ immigration; increased social mixing and ease of travel; changes to the education system (such as the effective abolition for UK residents of university tuition fees between 1962 and 1998, along with an introduction of maintenance grants in the 1960s). Here, I use the term 'working class' to refer to the relational identity of those people who might define themselves or be perceived as working class, acknowledging the 'leakiness'[10] of the term. This useage relates to Murray and his collaborators' explorations of class across each of the plays, which indicate the multiple ways that the working-class identity is experienced, and deal with issues of race, culture, economics, education, occupation and housing to demonstrate the complexity of class across a variety of fields and capitals.

To return to Beats & Elements then: issues of representation were what led Cree and Murray to create the company. They were also acutely aware of the particular class inequities existing in the theatre at the time, and their concurrent invisibility in wider discussions about inequality (indeed, class inequities continue in the theatre industry and elsewhere at the time of writing, although now with increased visibility due to the work of Murray, Cree and others in drawing attention to class injustice), which tended to focus on issues such as gender, race and disability – issues which are of course further exacerbated by class inequity. As a *Guardian* article written in the lead up to the company's first show *No Milk for the Foxes* suggests, the theatre industry is beset by class inequality in every sphere: among audiences, theatre makers, and gatekeepers such as Artistic Directors and executive boards:

> [. . .] the Warwick Commission found that the wealthiest, best educated and least ethnically diverse 8% of the population made up 28% of theatre audiences. Recent analysis of the Great British Class Survey discovered that only 10% of actors came from a working-class background – and those who did earned on average £10,000 a year less than their peers.[11]

For Beats & Elements, addressing issues of class needed to include addressing issues of representation. This meant not only having working-class people leading companies, writing and performing stories, but finding forms through which working-class stories could be told in all their complexity.

*No Milk for the Foxes*, written and performed by Murray and Cree and first staged in 2015, experimented with working-class forms. It did this through both the aesthetic choices made in the writing and staging, and through the creative process. Intertwining hip hop with a soap-opera-like realism, the play used working-class dialect, beatbox and rap to give an account of life on zero-hours contracts,[12] in an environment where workers' rights have been stripped back and working-class people are pitted against one another in the scramble for jobs and wages by which they might survive. The play cleverly weaves a critique of neoliberalism, and the difficulties of life for all working-class people, with a mediation on race. The character Mark embodies concerns that might be considered 'white working class'[13] – he wants to get by through hard work in a conventional job with regular hours, and understands that the decline of the trade unions, along with a lack of respectable jobs for working-class men, have contributed to his circumstances. He is a frustrated and unconfident version of white masculinity. His colleague Sparx, a mixed race, Anglo-Indian who speaks in Multicultural London English,[14] epitomises a generation of working-class Londoners, perhaps more detached from the histories of class struggle in the UK, and more willing to accept the current state of affairs as the way things are. Hip hop was the ideal form through which to tell this story, not only because both performers had already developed a language and voice in hip hop, but because it clearly signalled the working-class, multicultural roots of the company. As Murray notes in an interview printed later in this volume, hip hop forms emerge from working-class people living in multicultural neighbourhoods, where those struggling to survive in conditions of economic humiliation and hardship have found ways to express themselves and tell the stories of their lives. But the more realist aspects of this play speak to working-class culture too, telling the kinds of workplace and domestic stories that have been associated with working-class lives through such popular forms as kitchen sink realism and soap opera – which have significant histories of both working-class authorship and viewership.

*No Milk for the Foxes* was devised through a collaborative process (expanded in the interview on page 131 of this anthology), which might also be understood as rooted in working-class culture, where collective action (through unionisation and community organising, but also informal methods of collective child care and sharing domestic labour) has served as a means of survival and pride. In an overarching social, cultural and political system where individual success is often lauded, and where the collective labour that always produces creative work is effaced in favour of the creation of 'star' names, collaborative writing might be framed as a working-class method, capable of pushing against the prevailing norms of the entertainment industry.

In this collection, *No Milk for the Foxes* sits alongside *DenMarked*, a play Murray devised with the Battersea Arts Centre while also developing *No Milk*. Although it was not developed under the Beats & Elements company, *DenMarked* also speaks to and from the working-class experience, using hip hop and methods of collaboration (Murray worked with a wider creative team, credited in the play text) to tell a personal story rooted in class struggle. This play deals with issues of family, and the emotional complexity tied up in dysfunctional familial relations, which are themselves produced by poverty, humiliation and stress. The class struggle presented here is rooted in the domestic sphere, as much of the play deals with Murray's experiences of abuse, domestic violence and social care as a child growing up on a council estate in London. Unlike the exploitative reality televisions shows I mention above, *DenMarked* gives space to the humanity of those involved in class-produced dysfunction, and offers room for their complexity.

*DenMarked* served as something of a flashpoint in Murray's career. Used to devising with an ensemble of performers, in this solo work Murray was able to experiment with new musical techniques and to push his own abilities in beatbox, singing and rap further than might have been possible in an ensemble production. As he has noted elsewhere, however, the input of other people during this solo process offered a means by which to improve his practice.

Indeed, the concept of personal and community improvement through sharing and practising with others is important in hip hop culture.[15] This is perhaps most clearly demonstrated through the cypher, which is a tradition of sharing work in an informally competitive but non-combative manner, where each person offers their skills and talents to the collective. In the cypher, members stand in a circle, with each person taking turns to step forward and perform, showing what they have got to impress and inspire the next performance. Hyping up each performer with applause, verbal encouragement and vocal praise is common in cypher performances. By watching, listening, responding and performing to your peers in this way, it is possible to develop your own technique and to become better through practise. The 'battle' form similarly drives improvement in hip hop culture, although it is more formally competitive (and sometimes more combative) than the cypher. In a battle (usually) two performers will take it in turns to use their skills to impress an audience – the winner will commonly be chosen by the loudest audience applause and go on to battle another competitor. Although this may seem an individualist pursuit, the battle is also a means of collective practice – most battles take place in community venues where friends, neighbours and colleagues gather to share space with one another. The presence of an audience of peers and friends provides a supportive and nurturing environment in which to hone and develop skills. On those occasions where battles are more combative than nurturing, they provide a means of resolving conflicts without violence. And even if you lose, there is always the chance to come back next time and prove yourself. It may seem high-stakes in the moment, but battles are usually low-stakes in the greater scheme of life, and part of a good-natured spirit of learning and improving a craft alongside a group of talented peers with similar interests and shared experiences.

The concept of improvement runs through the process for the third work in this volume, *High Rise eState of Mind*, an ensemble piece devised and written by Beats & Elements with associate artists Lakeisha Lynch-Stevens and David Bonnick Jr. For this project, the group worked together, using J. G. Ballard's novel *High-Rise* as a stimulus for a show that reflects on the consequences of the housing crisis for young working-class Londoners – a group sometimes known as 'generation rent'. (In fact, Murray states that his inspiration on reading the book was to 'improve' the original story.) The process for developing *High Rise eState of Mind* included shared writing exercises, where the group would write in a studio, each producing verses to a prompt and a piece of originally composed music and performing these back to each other. As they explain later in this book, this led to a friendly competitive atmosphere, as each company member would push to create the most impressive verses, and later to improve the verses written by their collaborators in performance. The dextrous, creative and lyrically complex script is testimony to the efficacy of this approach, and to what can be achieved when modes of competition are used to encourage and develop one another, rather than as a means to undermine and establish hierarchies.

*High Rise eState of Mind* is concerned with the nature of destructive hierarchies and their consequences for class injustice. Developed in the wake of the horrific Grenfell Tower fire, in which seventy-two people (most of them working-class ethnic minorities) living in a tower block in west London died following a catastrophic series of building safety failures, the piece is alive to the extremely real and grim consequences of housing injustice for working-class people. Weaving the fictional story of life in a tower block where residents are segregated onto different floors due to wealth, the play comments on the current state of the London housing market, where the development of economically and socially stratified residences is becoming common. In a particularly famous example, the 'sky pool' – a transparent swimming pool that sits at the roof level of the Embassy Gardens development near Battersea (the district where, incidentally, *High Rise* was created) – is available only to those living in the most expensive apartments.[16] In *High Rise*, as each character navigates the oppressive system, struggling to rise to the top or simply to stay where they are, the performers step out of character and offer the audience stories from their real lives. In this way the play uses hip hop traditions of autobiography and realness or 'authenticity', to highlight how the housing system impacts lives in various ways. The power of the production lies not only in the wit and skill of the rhymes and lyrics, but in the way it encourages audiences to connect the fiction of the story to a wider political reality. In doing so, the play, like all the texts in this volume, attempts to contribute to the improvement of society in the realm of class justice.

## Notes

1  Owen Jones, *Chavs: The Demonisation of the Working Class* (London: Verso 2011).

2  The 'four elements' of hip hop are emceeing (or rapping), deejaying, breakdance and graffiti, although other elements, such as knowledge (often considered the 'fifth element'), style, beatboxing, sampling, remixing and authenticity are also key to hip hop culture. You can read more about the elements and how they have been used in Murray's work with TdC, Beatbox Academy and Beats & Elements in Katie Beswick and Conrad Murray, *Making Hip Hop Theatre: Beatbox and Elements* (London: Bloomsbury Methuen 2022).

3  See for example: Beverley Skeggs, *Formations of Class and Gender* (London: SAGE 1997); Anita Biressi and Heather Nunn, *Class and Contemporary British Culture* (Basingstoke: Palgrave Macmillan 2013); Imogen Tyler, *Stigma: The Machinery of Inequality* (London: Verso 2020).

4  See for example, Tracey Jensen, 'Welfare commonsense, poverty, porn and doxosophy', *Sociological Research Online* 19:3, pp. 277–83 (2014).

5  Katie Beswick, 'Capitalist realism: Glimmers, working-class authenticity and Andrea Dunbar in the twenty-first century', *International Journal of Media and Cultural Politics* 16:1, pp. 75–89 (2020).

6  Matt Trueman, 'No Milk for the Foxes: The beatboxing show bringing council estate rage to the theatre', *The Guardian* (22 April 2015) available at: https://www.theguardian.com/stage/2015/apr/22/no-milk-for-the-foxes-beatboxing-theatre-council-estate-class-beats-elements [accessed 8 June 2021].

7  BBC 'Profile: John Prescott' (August 2007) available at: http://news.bbc.co.uk/1/hi/uk_politics/6636565.stm [accessed 9 June 2021].

8  Pierre Bourdieu, *Distinction: A Social Critique of the Judgement of Taste* (London: Routledge 1984).

9  David Morgan, *Snobbery* (Bristol: Policy Press 2018).

10 Beverley Skeggs, 'The Making of Class and Gender through Visualizing Moral Subject Formation', *Sociology* 39:5, pp. 965–82 (2005).

11 Trueman, 'No Milk for the Foxes' (2015).
12 See for example, Nikhil Datta, Giulia Giupponi and Stephen Machin 'Zero-hours contracts and labour market policy' *Economic Policy* 34:99, pp. 369–427 (2020).
13 To reflect further on what it might mean to embody a 'white working class' identity see: Lisa McKenzie, 'On the frontline: Left out. The other "other" ', *Discover Society* (4 March 2014) available at: https://archive.discoversociety. org/2014/03/04/on-the-frontline-left-out-the-other-other/ [accessed 9 June 2021] and Simon Winlow and Steve Hall *The Rise of the Right: English Nationalism and The Transformation of Working-Class Politics* (Bristol: Policy Press 2016).
14 Or 'MLE' a London dialect spoken by people of all races that combines multicultural influences such as Jamaican Patois and Cockney, often associated with working-class youth.
15 Raphael Travis Jnr., *The Healing Power of Hip Hop* (Westport: Praeger 2015).
16 Tom Ravenscroft, 'Fully transparent Sky Pool provides "a swim like no other" between two housing blocks in London', *dezeen* (4 June 2021) available at: https://www.dezeen.com/2021/06/04/transparent-swimming-pool-battersea-london-hal-sky-pool/ [accessed 9 July 2021].

# Hip Hop Lyricism

Numerous scholars and practitioners across the globe, but particularly scholars of colour in the USA, including Daniel Banks,[1] Nicole Hodges Persley,[2] Bakari Kitwana[3] and Tricia Rose[4] have shown the important insights that are generated by treating hip hop forms as serious objects of inquiry. By taking hip hop and its attendant politics seriously in their own scholarship, these thinkers have paved the way for others who understand the critical and social possibilities of the form. Here, I want to build on existing scholarship by taking seriously the literary value of hip hop and the potentials for reading hip hop as literature, using the works in this anthology. This is by no means an original line of inquiry. The fact that hip hop is a powerful literary as well as popular cultural form is now widely accepted, despite the snobbery that still exists towards non-canonical forms and colloquial language and dialect.[5] Scholars, cultural commentators and hip hop heads worldwide have dedicated time to making the case for hip hop's literary merit and to analysing and unpacking the complex and layered meanings of rap lyrics and performance.[6]

In the UK, rapper and cultural critic Akala is probably the most prominent proponent of rap as literature. He points out how hip hop shares similarities to Shakesperian verse, and his work in articulating the literary value of rap verses has been influential in the fields of both Shakespeare and hip hop.[7] Practitioners working with young people and in community and educational settings have adopted Akala's insights to emphasise the contemporary relevance of canonical literature, as well as to convince the literary elite of rap's specific value.[8] Meanwhile, the website Rap Genius (now rebranded as, simply, 'Genius' and spanning multiple genres) created a forum for rap fans everywhere to post lyrics, annotate them and to offer interpretations, providing an everyday form of literary analysis whose popularity is a testament to the potentials of textual analysis in the world outside academia. The popularity of Rap Genius suggests the importance of lyrism as a mode of enjoyment, connection and fulfilment, and evidences the literary attention rap fans pay to the music. Making sense of words is not just an elite academic process, but fundamental to the way many of us engage with language and use it to enrich our social relationships.

Lyricism is the poetic power of language. Indeed, the word lyricism, which is often summoned when discussing hip hop music, encompasses both the literary techniques that structure hip hop language and the affective or 'feeling' dimensions of such language. In other words, lyricism is the complex process by which techniques such as metaphor, simile, analogy, narrative, personification and so on create meaning and produce emotions for the listener or reader. For those of us who enjoy words in one form or another (which is to say most everyone who has ever been moved by a song, poem, novel, play or film) language has the power to create particular kinds of pleasure – not only through transmitting direct meanings that are connected to specific memories or relay particular events, but also via kinaesthetic pleasures created by rhythm and meter, as well as through abstracted and layered sounds and images. Words, whether spoken or written, on their own or in combination with other words, can work through the body, creating sensations which, like those described by Joslin McKinney in her discussion of visual spectacles, are almost beyond articulation.[9] Perhaps the sensual and powerful feelings created by a particularly lyrical combination of words come close to what Audre Lorde is getting at in her essay, 'Uses of the Erotic'. Lorde describes the powerful, feminine energy that works on a bodily and often subconscious level to stimulate our deepest knowledge of ourselves:

> The erotic is a measure between the beginnings of our sense of self and the chaos of our strongest feelings. It is the internal sense of satisfaction to which, once we have experienced it, we know we can aspire. For having experienced the fullness of this depth of feeling and recognising its power, in honor and self-respect we can require no less of ourselves.[10]

In hop hop terms, we might consider Lorde's erotic within the frame of 'knowledge' – that vital 'fifth' element of the culture which asks us to be aware of injustice, connected to our deepest truths and awake and alert to one another. Like Lorde's erotic, hip hop knowledge acknowledges the power we hold within ourselves to connect to the deepest mysteries of the universe, as well as to make practical and pragmatic changes in the world which might address systems of injustice and inequity, especially in the realms of racism and classism. Rap lyricism is a means of accessing the erotic. If this seems a somewhat oblique way into understanding the operation of rap as literature, that it is because I believe that the sensuous and attendant spiritual dimensions of our experience are vital to acknowledge and harness in any struggle for a full life or for social and political change. As bell hooks argues, a 'love ethic', by which we bring our own light to our endeavours and encourage luminosity in others, has fuelled many social justice movements as well as characterising the most radical aspects of religious and spiritual teachings.[11] Through approaching hip hop as a global project of love and opening ourselves to the powerful possibilities of being moved by its language, we might also find ways of connecting to and understanding one another in an increasingly divided and hostile world.

In the plays in this volume, we can approach analysis of the language to think about how lyricism works through multiple layers. The works here are complex, using narrative story-telling techniques, dialogue, rhyme, cadence and specific word choices to transmit a politics that is deeply rooted in feeling. As in much hip hop, the feeling energy is also located in a specific time and place[12] – here it is contemporary south London. By reading the works and paying attention to their complexity we might derive a particular kind of pleasure as well as find connection with the writers or speakers – certain kinds of lyricism allow us to see things from a new point of view and so to change our perspective. But because the language of hip hop is often rooted in diasporic, street and non-standard dialect, which is highly localised, it can be difficult to deduce the complexity of meaning for listeners or readers who are not intimately acquainted with local dialect and expression. This may be why hip hop forms are still treated with derision by those members of the literary elite who see little beauty in working-class expression (likely because they do not care to spend time understanding it). Nonetheless, appreciating the complexity of slang and local dialect and accent – taking seriously the literary potential street-talk and working-class ways of speaking afford – can offer greater pleasure and open texts up to richer and more profound meanings.

In *High Rise eState of Mind* (perhaps the most lyrical of the works collected here) there are many examples of lyricism that give us as readers insight into both the characters' and the performers' world-views. A moment of word-play that I was struck by mid-way through the action happens in the song 'How Long?' At this point in the play, Michelle and Luke's relationship fractures and Michelle, desperate to ascend to a higher floor of the Mark One tower block where they live, makes a phone call to enquire about employment opportunities. In her verse, Michelle narrates how she is fobbed off by the bureaucrats who take her call. She describes her frustration with the process in a witty rhyme:

Hung up – what a fucking bellyache,
It's too early for a mug when
I've barely even ate.

The term 'mug' has multiple meanings in informal south London vernacular, and more generally in formal English, which can be deduced from context to make meaning of the lines. By unpacking the layers of meaning encapsulated in a single word, it is possible to give some insight into the complicated and clever way that rap works to produce lyrical pleasure. Here, 'mug' follows 'bellyache', which is a London slang term for 'annoying or protracted event'. Michelle's morning has been ruined by a protracted phone call, ended when the man on the other end of the line hangs up on her. 'Mug' in this context has a double meaning: it is both a cup you drink breakfast tea from and an idiotic or extremely annoying person. In the rhyme above, mug is therefore employed as a noun (the adjectival form of the insult would be 'muggy', as in 'muggy cunt', a common south London slur). This second meaning (idiot/annoying) is perhaps derived from the rhyming slang 'mug and spoon' for 'loon' or 'lunatic'(sometimes 'cup and spoon'): a crazy person, or someone who makes you feel crazy or angry. Over time, its usage has evolved to generally indicate someone you disrespect, or find idiotic and annoying. Another common slang noun usage of 'mug' is as a synonym for 'face', especially an unattractive one (as in 'look at your ugly mug'), or one appearing close-up in a photograph ('mugshot') – this also works as a verb ('to mug' is 'to pull a silly face'). 'Mug' can also be used in slang as a verb to mean taken for a fool, tricked or taken advantage of ('to mug' or to be 'taken for a mug', or to 'mug off'). You might also use this in a noun form (as in, 'what a mug he is'/'don't I feel a mug'), to indicate someone who has been taken for a fool, easily deceived or behaved foolishly, or to indicate your own embarrassment at having been fooled (this likely comes from a formal meaning of mug as verb form, as in to be 'mugged' or stolen from in a public place) – this meaning has some cultural dominance due to its frequent invocation in the television series *The Only Way is Essex* ('You mug!'). In the *High Rise* lyrics, 'it's too early for a mug', Michelle is saying it is too early in the day to deal with someone who is very annoying, but creates humour with the reference to rhyming slang where mug is also a vessel for drinking breakfast tea. Other interpretations of the lyric which rely on different meanings of the word mug might lose the grammatical logic of the line and the rhyming slang word-play, but might still make sense in the logic of the song, or impinge on and add texture to this primary meaning (e.g. that Michelle feels taken for a mug or fobbed off/embarrassed; that the man on the phone is ugly/foolish). The complexity of that single word in Michelle's rhyme gives some idea of the possibility of lyricism for creating enjoyment for audiences – the more you understand the complexity of the language and the many possible meanings, the more pleasure you might derive from the rhymes and what they tell us about the characters and their situation.[13] This of course means that the reader or listener must use their own knowledge and experience to interpret the words, and that the meaning and feeling created by a particular lyric, verse or song may be hyper-local, and extremely personal to the individual interpreter. In this way, lyricism connects to knowledge, as it encourages us to actively go inward, working through our personal connection with someone else's words to make sense of the world.

My experience of the song 'Cotchin'' in *DenMarked* offers an insight into the ways our personal histories and specific knowledge might shape our interpretation of a song. The word 'cotchin'' or 'cotching' is slang for 'resting', 'idling' or 'lying down' and is famously used by Dizzee Rascal on the track 'Dream', where he raps about 'cotching on the stairs in the flats'. This Dizzee lyric refers to the way that groups of young people sit in the stairwells of council estate tower blocks, idling around when there is little else to do. When Conrad raps about 'cotchin'' it evoked the lyric in 'Dream' for me, as someone very familiar with that song, but also reminded me of my friends growing up, who had also used the word to describe relaxing or idling. It evoked strong feelings associated with the past, and sensations of being in and around council housing. Because it connected to memories from my past, the lyric was able to produce a specific and highly personal nostalgic response for me – which may or may not be shared by other listeners. In this instance my own experiences collided with the lyric to enhance my understanding and sensuous encounter with the play.

In *No Milk for the Foxes* the character name 'Sparx' works in a similarly complex way to tell us something about the character and to convey a set of feelings about the context he inhabits. Marks and Sparks is a colloquial name for the British retailer Marks and Spencer, and Mark is Sparx's sidekick in *No Milk*. However, when read on the page – particularly in the context of a play about the working-class experience – the name Sparx also suggests the name of the writer Karl Marx, one of the authors of *The Communist Manifesto*, whose work theorised the exploitation of the working classes. The fact that this link to Marx is only possible to deduce when the name is written down indicates the importance of rap lyrics existing in both a physical and aural form (as anyone who has hunted for the lyrics printed in the album cover of cds might attest). In both spoken and written form the name Sparx also evokes the London slang word for an electrician, 'spark' suggesting a manual labouring background. It might also be a tongue-in-cheek reference to Sparx's lack of formal education and naivety (the slang word for an educated person also being 'spark' or 'bright spark', often used sarcastically to mean the opposite). Given that Mark and Sparx are both victims of the capitalist system, the layering of working-class imagery in Sparx's name serves as a reminder of the class politics that runs throughout *No Milk*, and which structure both the characters' and the performers' lives.

These brief attempts at parsing the lyricism of the plays in this volume offer a starting point for readers to think with the texts that follow. There is much more to be said, for example about the pleasure of word sounds, as well as their meanings, that I don't have time to expand in this essay. Publishing this anthology is a means of taking seriously the possibilities of hip hop theatre as dramatic literature. The hope is that readers will find their own pleasure in the plays, and use their personal experiences and enhance their knowledge by analysing the language and developing critical and creative responses to the texts. Language is a cultural, social and political means of communication and we can harness its power to better understand ourselves and the world, and to make changes. However you approach the plays that follow (whether as a reader, theatre maker, student, hip hop head or sceptic), I suggest that you allow yourself to be moved by the language, and to enjoy making meaning from the words – remember that your unique experiences and perspectives on the world mean you are also collaborating in the creation of the plays as you read them.

## Notes

1   Daniel Banks, *Say Word! Voices from Hip Hop Theater* (Ann Arbor: University of Michigan Press 2011).
2   Nicole Hodges Persley, *Sampling and Re-Mixing Blackness in Hip Hop Theater and Performance* (Ann Arbor: University of Michigan Press 2021).
3   Bakari Kitwana, *The Hip Hop Generation: Young Blacks and the Crisis in African American Culture* (New York: Basic Civitas Books 2002).
4   Tricia Rose, *Black Noise: Rap Music and Black Culture in Contemporary America* (Middletown: Wesleyan University Press 1994).
5   Lauren Leigh Kelly, 'Hip-Hop Literature: The Politics, Poetics and Power of Hip-Hop in the English Classroom', *The English Journal* 102:5, pp. 51–6.
6   See for example: Sarah Little, 'Women, ageing, and Hip Hop: Discourses and imageries of ageing femininity', *Feminist Media Studies* 18:1, pp. 34–46 (2018); and Sarah Simeziane, 'Roma rap and the *Black Train*: Minority voices in Hungarian hip hop' in Marina Terkourafi (ed.), *Languages of Hip Hop* (London and New York: Continnuum 2010) pp. 96–119.
7   Stephen O'Neill, '"It's William Back from the Dead": Commemoration, Representation, and Race in Akala's Hip-Hop Shakespeare', *Studies in Ethnicity and Nationalism* 16:2, pp. 246–56 (2016).
8   See for example, 'Akala and hip hop Shakespeare'. Available at: https://www.folger.edu/shakespeare-unlimited/akala-hip-hop-shakespeare [accessed 22 July 2021].
9   Joslin McKinney, 'Scenography, Spectacle and the Body of the Spectator', *Performance Research* 18:3, pp. 63–74 (2013).
10  Audre Lorde, 'Uses of the Erotic: The Erotic as Power', in *Your Silence Will Not Protect You* (London: Silver Press 2017) p. 23.
11  bell hooks, *All About Love New Visions* (New York: William Morrow 2000).
12  Murray Forman, *The 'Hood Comes First: Race, Space and Place in Rap and Hip Hop* (Middletown: Wesleyan University Press 2002).
13  This analysis of the term 'mug' appears in a slightly different form in Katie Beswick, '*High Rise eState of Mind*: love and honesty in the midst of London's neoliberal housing crisis', *Comparative Drama* (2021).

# No Milk for the Foxes

**Paul Cree and Conrad Murray**

First performed at Camden People's Theatre on 22 April 2015.

Recordings of some of the tracks for this performance are available on YouTube, Apple Music, Spotify and SoundCloud.

## Character List (original cast)

**Mark**   *Twenties–thirties white working-class man* (Paul Cree)
**Sparx**  *Twenties–thirties Anglo-Indian working-class man* (Conrad Murray)

## Creative Team

*Dramaturgical Advisor*   Tom Parkinson
*Lighting Designer*       Simeon Miller
*Producer*                Lara Taylor
*Set Designer*            Rosalind Russell

## Scene One

**Mark** *enters, and starts cleaning and setting up the office.* **Sparx** *takes jacket off aggressively, and then turns the office light off.*

**Mark**    What you doing?

**Sparx**    Got a fucking headache, innit?

**Mark**    Five sugars, yeah?

**Sparx**    Sweet.

*Pause.*

How's that hole in the fence man? Has it got any bigger? Has anyone like, broken through and that?

**Mark**    Nah, not yet. But I reckon it's got bigger since the last time I checked.

**Sparx**    What, since yesterday?

**Mark**    Yeah. And I mentioned it to Wayne last night for the security report. And just to make sure, I then stuck it in an email to him explaining in more detail on why I thought it posed a potential threat . . . There's a fire exit twenty-nine metres from that hole.

**Sparx**    Twenty-nine metres?

**Mark**    Yep, twenty-nine metres – which leads right onto the factory floor, anyone could get in there and have thousands of pounds worth of components away . . . Oi, Wayne said 'well done' for being vigilant.

**Sparx**    Twenty-nine metres . . . like . . . How do you know it's twenty-nine metres?

**Mark**    Why does it matter?

**Sparx**    Cos it does!

**Mark**    Because you want to take the piss? Look, in one of them old cupboards I found some stationary. I sellotaped three thirty centimetres rulers together with one ten centimetre ruler, then went outside and measured twenty-nine meters in the rain!

**Sparx**    Fucking hell, man. Did you get a Blue Peter badge for that? Don't give up your day job will you mate?

**Mark**    This IS my day job mate.

**Sparx**    It's a night shift, there aren't no day jobs around here!

**Mark**    Alright. Whatever.

**Sparx**    I don't know why you're so concerned about the hole in the fence anyway. It's not like there's a fucking black market for washing machine circuit boards is there? Someone going round teefing washing machine circuit board parts bruv? Unless that hole isn't a hole, it's actually a black hole to another dimension and you're like the sworn fucking protector of the galaxy with your Maglite torch and your notepad bruv! There's videos about people like you on YouTube man.

**Mark**    I'm sure there is, bruv, I'm sure there is. Look, if anything, there's lead on the roof, that stuff's getting robbed left right and centre, apparently you can get good money for it at scrap yards.

**Sparx**    Yeah you could, but the price has gone down ain't it? Not even worth it.

**Sparx** *flicks through* The Sun *newspaper.*

What happened to page three man? What is this like? Fucking boring.

**Sparx** *throws the newspaper in the bin.*

**Mark**    Oi what you doing?

**Sparx**    I've read it innit?

**Mark**    Mate that's mine. I need that.

**Sparx**    What for?

**Mark**    Saving up for holiday tokens.

**Sparx**    Butlin's, yeah?

**Mark**    No. Went to Butlin's last year . . . It was sick . . . Me and Gemma are saving up to go to the south of France.

**Sparx**    South of France bruv?

**Mark**    Yep.

**Sparx**    You?

**Mark**    Yeah.

**Sparx**    You do know like, the sun shines down there don't you? It gets hot and that?

**Mark**   Yep.

**Sparx**   You've got pasty skin man, you get a sunburn when you switch the fucking light on! You better watch that.

**Mark**   Ha. Ha. Very funny. It's alright for you, you don't know what it's like.

**Sparx**   Like, what do you mean, 'You don't know what it's like?'

**Mark**   Well, you're like half Black or whatever, you're used to it.

**Sparx**   Half Indian actually! And I'll have you know that I do suffer from sunstroke and or sunburn from time to time. And so do some Black people. You better watch it with them casual racist comments there man.

**Mark**   Look I'm sorry bruv, I didn't mean to cause offence I'm just saying that like, you're like darker skinned than me so you can tolerate the sun more that's all.

**Sparx**   It's alright. I've had it my whole life. I'm still kinda pissed at you, for them UKIP BNP statements you keep making there. So like to make it up to me, I'm gonna let you do like the next four rounds. Maybe five. It's up to you. To make it up to me.

**Mark**   But hold on, like, you started it. You were cussing me for being pale, that's racist innit?

**Sparx**   It's not the same man.

**Mark**   Why?

**Sparx**   Cos it ain't . . . Bruv I know about you people. Googled that shit: reptiles, lizards, Columbus, colonialism, Coldplay, coca-cola, DAVID CAMERON!

**Mark**   Bruv I see you drinking coca-cola all the time. And you probably like Coldplay.

**Sparx**   Nah nah nah.

**Mark**   What's that all got to do with me anyway?

**Sparx**   You're one of THEM bruv.

**Mark**   Yeah, but how does that work? And aren't you half white anyway?

**Sparx**    Bruv, what did I tell you about those fucking racist comments you're making there?

**Sparx** *is banging on his phone, frustrated.*

Checking my account over and over again and that. There's no pay in there, there's no p's and that . . . No fucking p's.

**Mark**    Same, checked it this morning.

**Sparx**    I checked my pingit app over and over again like, I'm gonna fucking call Wayne bruv.

**Mark**    Yeah.

**Sparx**    Like, where's this dough, I'm gonna tell him bruv. Fucking clown!

**Mark**    You asked him about the hole?

**Sparx** *bangs hard on the phone buttons.*

Yo, Wayne!

*He immediately changes his delivery, to soft and well spoken.*

Yeah . . . It's Steven. Basically, it was about my pay. I . . . I'm checking my account over and over again and. . . . Ok. I gave her my time sheets. So, nothing's gonna go in then, no? Oh . . . Ok. Thanks. Next time yeah? Thanks Wayne.

*Hangs up*

FUCKING DICKHEAD BRUV! Dickhead.

**Mark**    What?

**Sparx**    Well didn't you fucking just hear me? I said 'Where's my fucking dough bruv?' I said, 'Where's my fucking paper like?', and he still weren't letting up.

**Mark**    Alright. What's happened? What did he say?

**Sparx**    He said we are definitely not getting paid this week.

**Mark**    Right.

**Sparx**    Apparently that fucking bitch in the office, Louise, worked a half day on Friday, so because of that we ain't getting paid. Even though I did what I'm supposed to do, I put my fucking time sheets in bruv.

**Mark**    Calm down, this happens all the time, don't worry.

**Sparx**  Nah, I'm leaving bruv. I'm quitting, that's it. This is you. This fucking shit is YOU bruv. Look around this place innit? Think about it, round here it's full of pussies and dickheads bruv. Which one are you?

**Mark** *doesn't say anything.*

**Sparx**  Dickhead!

**Mark**  What are you doing? You can't leave! What are you gonna do? Go on JSA?

**Sparx**  JSA! What you think I can't fucking do that? Oh what, fill in those boxes like, 'Oh yeah. Man was looking for a job on Monday, I went on Google on fucking Tuesday.' You think I can't do that? I'll even sit in one of those centres, where you read old fucking newspapers circling jobs that went three months ago – drinking cold tea. You think I ain't fucking done that over and over again? Fuck this shit bruv.

**Mark**  Listen. Bruv, all jobs are like this now. You'll get the dough eventually. JSA ain't much better, they take ages to pay. Look, I know we ain't got it, but we will get it. They normally pay on time. You can get to buy your trainers every month and pay your bills. And bruv, you don't even do much. What more do you want?

**Sparx**  MORE!

'Stuck' *Rap Interlude one*

*Verse 1 –* **Mark**

If you're stuck in a rut and you're feeling low
but you smoke loads of weed and you watch all the soaps
and you wanna know why it hasn't happened for you
that, that talent and passion has not made money for you
because you didn't ever actually apply yourself
you never took a risk so you denied yourself
so know you wanna play puppet for lacking the possibilities
without ever taking any opportunities
can't understand this individualism whatever happened to living in
    unison
the unions had the backs of our dads and our mums had the church
and all the greed and credit was deemed the devil's work
now it's information instant gratification
and if you make a mistake, then 'you must be mistaken'
because you can't lose face, in any situation
can't remember the last time I waved at my neighbours

*Verse 2 –* **Sparx**

Going to the job centre making up job activities
that I'm supposed to be searching for weekly
regularly but they don't do nothing for me
hands me this little pen and says 'sign something for me'
what else can I do to prove to you
that over ten years I went off to school
tried to follow the rules teachers couldn't teach,
I'm trying to see the future but is out of my reach
I'm feeling kinda stressed, feeling depressed
I never got those jobs they didn't like the way I dressed
I'm fucking broke can hardly afford to smoke,
it's a fucking joke man
it's a fucking joke

**'It's England'** *Rap Interlude two*

*Verse 1 –* **Mark**

There's food in my belly there's a roof on my head
and when I wake in the morning a pretty woman in my bed
yes we live with my parents but these days who doesn't
we'll get married, get a place and have a couple of young'ens
it's alright I'm doing fine I got a wage coming in
and with the way things are going I'm pretty lucky to live
if I get my nut down I'll see a difference in digits
as I climb up the ladder I'll get a better payslip

It's England, apparently everything's shit
It's England, apparently everything's shit
It's England, apparently everything's shit
It's England, apparently everything's shit

*Verse 2 –* **Sparx**

Yo, logging, clocking, enter the data
we used to have dreams but now we're off of the radar
it would have been better if I was in prison
at least I can see my bars
sleeping down at the curb staring up at night
you can see the stars,
staring at computer screens zoning out
sticking to the rules means were cloning out

we were already austere round here
but they ain't never ever been round here
so
stick to the program
you be happy if you stick to the program
why don't you just stick to the program
and everybody just stick to the program.


**Scene Two**

**Mark**  Bruv, I've been robbed untold times on them tubes late at night, them machines ain't gonna stop that.

**Sparx**  They should be sacked like, each and every fucking one of em. Fucking sacked. I've gotta come to work, like, why they don't go to work? Any excuse now. Any fucking excuse.

**Mark**  Nah mate. It's unions looking out for their people. What's that big geezer's name? 'Bob' Something? Bob. . . .? Bob Crow, that's the guy! They're sticking up for guys like us mate!

**Sparx**  Nah, I ain't having a bar of it bruv, like 'Unions?' Yeah? Unions. David Cameron, the government? You know that's the same thing, innit?

**Mark**  Mate, if we were in the unions, I'm pretty sure we wouldn't be having these issues getting paid and me and you might actually have a proper fixed term contracts, pensions, holiday, sick pay, all of that.

**Sparx**  Bruv, what fucking planet are you living at? Contracts? Sick pay? Pensions? Shit don't change.

**Mark**  Bruv, my grandad was in the union.

**Sparx**  Is it?

**Mark**  For years. He worked on the railroads and the unions looked after him. They used to have these social clubs that you would go to on the weekends. They have like full-size snooker tables. They do discos, and family days down to the coast. That was great. And anyway, last shift I worked with you, you were banging on all night about going on strike!

**Sparx**  That's different, innit? When I say 'I'm gonna go on strike' I fucking mean it innit! Like, I gonna go on fucking strike. I don't need a fucking gang bruv. I'm one man up! I don't need no fucking, fucking Masons no illuminati, no union. Like, backing my arse up. Like, what's this thing? Russell Crow? Helping me out and that? Nah bruv. 'Low that bruv. I do me. I'm independent.

*Beatbox section to indicate the passing of time.*


## Scene Three

**Mark** *is playing a game on his phone.*

**Mark**    Oh mate. . . . GO ON! Yeah.

**Sparx**    Bro what the fucking you looking at?

**Mark**    What me?

**Sparx**    Yeah man.

**Mark**    Oi, you ever played that game on Facebook? FarmVille? Ah man, it's the best, me and Gemma play it. You get to grow your own stuff on your own farm, and you sell it and make money.

**Sparx**    Bruv! You ACTUALLY fucking play THAT?

**Mark**    Yeah.

**Sparx**    Messing about with fake crops and that?

**Mark**    Yeah! It's the one mate!

**Sparx**    I don't need to mess around with fake fucking crops bruv. I know about real things like that bruv. I used to live with my grandparents innit?

**Mark**    Yeah?

**Sparx**    I had a teenage mum, so they kinda helped out and that. We planted (*kisses teeth*). We used to go down Tooting Bec Common picking raspberries man. They love planting things and that. And making things, bruv. They used to make me and my little brother little things out of pots, lollipop sticks and that. Not complicated. Little things bruv. All these fake shit? 'Low that. They're fucking old now though innit, like. Old. Now they just watch John Wayne *Rio Grande* and the *Searchers*. My nan hates John Wayne, she can't stand him. She calls my grandad, 'The Prune'. He calls her, 'Fat cow'. She always says, 'You ain't nice you are'. Bruv, it's mad. My grandad buys balloons for the dog right? He calls em ''loons' and he blows it up and he throws it to the dog. And the dog's like, biting at it, and scratching at it. Never pops a fucking balloon. Gardening? That's the thing they're into. They love seeing new things grow. 'Look at it!' And I don't even know what I'm looking at. They like rhubarb man. Like, what the fuck's rhubarb? I swear it's just for old people like. I look at that little plot like, it's everything to them. They talk about it for ages but there's nothing there. Piece of shit really. It's 2015 and they don't know about no fucking 'farmvilles', bruv. Twitter, Facebooks, none of that. Apple Macs and that? They know about real fucking apples! Nah bruv. To them it's just about gardens, balloons, and hours and hours of The Duke. It's a different world.

**Mark**    Look, come here! I'll show you yeah. Look . . . look. Gemma? She started growing satsumas, and now she's exporting to South America bruv!

**Sparx**    You on that thing like. Didn't you like playing real games and that?

**Mark**    Course I did!

**Sparx**    Running about and that?

**Mark**    Yeah!

**Sparx**    Man, did you ever go to like the coast and bang out the fruities and one armed bandits?

**Mark**    Course!

**Sparx**    You're a big man you know.

**Mark**    Yeah? Yeah! Big man yeah . . . I guess so bruv.

**Sparx**    Haven't you ever thought about getting serious?

**Mark**    Serious? Yeah . . . Yeah, serious, yeah.

**Sparx**    Serious with your paper bruv?

**Mark**    Yeah. Money? Yeah bruv, serious.

**Sparx**    That's what I'm talking about. What's to say that me and you don't start stacking dough bruv?

**Mark**    Me and you?

**Sparx**    Me and you bruv. Let's both save up a grand a piece.

**Mark**    A grand!?

**Sparx**    It'll take time man. We'll save up a grand and we'll flip that to five grand bruv!

**Mark**    Woah, hold on, five grand?

**Sparx**   Flip that dough bruv! Imagine that. Me and you, a grand just sitting there bruv. And we take that grand and we flip that to five grand. Are you on that ting bruv?

**Mark**   Me and you bruv!

**Sparx**   We take that grand and we're gonna go to Mecca Bingo bruv! FULL HOUSE! Flip that dough bruv!. . .

*Pause.*

**Mark**   Bingo?

**Sparx**   You didn't know about them tings there bruv? Man, its fucking easy. It's kinda easy, but its kinda complicated like. You go down there, and you have this pen and you are circling these numbers. It's coming at you kinda fast.You gotta catch it! But when you catch it, it's like 'Boom' flip that dough bruv! FULLHOUSE! I don't mess with that felt tip, for me, it's more the stamper thing, that's more my style. Stamping it and that bruv.

**Mark**   Bingo man? Yeah but, like, bingo? Ain't that like, gambling? Triumph without merit? That's like half of humanity mate.

**Sparx**   Trium . . . What the fuck are you talking about? How many hours did you work last week? How many hours are you gonna end up working this week? Next fucking week? We just worked all week and never got fucking paid! Gambling like? At least with fucking bingo we put down our fucking money bruv, and if we win we flip that dough! And if we lose? Well? At least we had a fucking choice in that. You don't get it man.

**Mark**   Bingo?

**Sparx**   My nan used to play every day innit?

*Beatbox and movement interlude to indicate the passing of time.*

**Scene Four**

**Mark**   How long have you worked here now?

**Sparx**   Ages man. Time! Been here for days.

**Mark**   Nah, you been here for about three weeks? And according to that, you were off for the whole week last week.

**Sparx**   I was sick the whole week. I was ill innit? Three weeks? All right, weeks.

**Mark**    See me bruv? I've been here for nine months four weeks three days and about five and a half hours. You're still wet behind the ears mate. What you reckon on Wayne?

**Sparx**    Dickhead!

**Mark**    Noooo. Wayne's alright. I was thinking right, we don't get to see him much, but I was like, if I got to know him a little bit better maybe he'll sort us out with some more shifts?

**Sparx**    Nah man. If you see how he goes on. Every Friday drinks bro, we don't even chat bruv! He's just banging down the Heineken. You know he's on the sniff don't ya? He's a fucking wild bruv, he's a nutter bruv! I wouldn't even . . . You don't wanna fuck with Wayne man.

**Mark**    Friday drinks?

**Sparx**    Ye . . . Yeah. Friday drinks like.

**Mark**    No. What Friday drinks?

**Sparx**    You know like every Friday? Well obviously like, you were saying, I been here for three weeks. You been here for three eons like obviously they're trying to get me to know the other workers like to fit me in bruv.You're stacking your dough now? Stacking all your dough? You're not spending money on that bruv. Know what I'm saying?

**Mark**    Alright. Seeing as you're a bit 'pally pally' with Wayne, has he ever mentioned anything about . . . about me? Or like us, getting proper contracts?

**Sparx**    Bruv, why are you coming to me with contracts and that?

**Mark**    I'm just asking.

**Sparx**    Wayne and contracts and that? It's like you know something.

**Mark**    No . . . I'm just . . .

**Sparx**    It's like you're coming at me, bruv. You're attacking man. You're coming at me with this shit bruv. You're attacking me. You think I know something. I'm supposed to know things?

**Mark**    No!

**Sparx**    Why are you coming at me man? It's like being attacked right now. That's how I feel in the workplace. I'm being attacked. You're victimising me, bruv! That's what's happening right now. Over and over again, asking me all this shit bruv? How am I supposed to know this shit? What kinda shit do I know? I don't know nothing. I can't take this shit no more. All right?! On Bowling Tuesday —

**Mark**    Bowling Tuesday??!

**Sparx**    Like, Wayne said something about hours being cut.

**Mark**    What. Hours being cut? What did he say?

**Sparx**    I just told you innit? You asked me and I told you. Hours getting cut. That's what I heard man.

**Mark**    Mate! This is important, what exactly did he say?

**Sparx**    He said something like . . . I don't even listen bruv. I weren't even listening to what he was saying. He says things. I don't even know what I'm fucking hearing. I don't even know what I'm saying. I don't know what I'm saying right now! You're coming at me.

**Mark**    If he's saying anything in the future, you will tell me yeah?

**Sparx**    What's the problem like?

**Mark**    Gemma's due next month mate. And I got to pay bills. This ain't enough. I need more shifts.

**'Gemma (never had)'** *Rap Interlude three*

*Chorus 1*

Never had them brand new clothes
Never had that holiday abroad
Always had that four stripe addias
Got abused by the kids at school
Never had them brand new clothes
Never had that holiday abroad
Always had that four stripe addias
Got abused by the kids at school

*Verse 1*

White letters started coming through the letter box
Telling me to apply for credit
Mum and Dad said don't get it
If it ain't your pocket then you ain't got it

*Chorus 2*

But I wanted them brand new clothes
And I wanted that holiday abroad

I wanted that three stripe addias
Never had it so I, wanted it all

*Verse 2*

White letters turned into red letters
Debt chasers calling my phone
Buried my head in the sand
Just wished that I'd listened to my folks
Gemma came along when I was in a mess
She helped me sort out my life
Took me down to citizens' advice
Helped me get my head right
We enjoy each other's company
We have a laugh, she thinks I'm funny
I tap her on the shoulder and, run away
She falls for it, so easily
She always leaves a third of her tea and only ever
Eats half of her biscuit
We both like sci-fi films
And both think *EastEnders* is shit
We don't spend much time together
I work nights and she works days but
Those few minutes in a day
Are always worth the wait

*Chorus 3*

I don't want them brand new clothes
Don't need that holiday abroad
I'm fine with four stripe addias
Just wanna spend time with Gemma more
I don't want them brand new clothes
Don't need that holiday abroad
I'm fine with four stripe addias
Just wanna spend time with Gemma more.

**Sparx**    What's Gemma like? You're always going on about 'Gemma'. 'Gemma' this 'Gemma' that. She's cool yeah?

**Mark**    She's great bruv. Real good. She works at reception at a finance company over in the city. She does alright. Doesn't earn loads of money, but funnily enough, her company had their annual works 'do' last week, so I was invited along as her plus one mate. Like proper plush do.

Whatcha call it? Black tie! So all the guys there were in dinner jackets. All the women were in cocktail dresses. I had to borrow a suit off my dad bruv.

**Sparx**    Bruv, was there free food there?

**Mark**    Oh mate, loads of free food.

**Sparx**    That's sick man!

**Mark**    All come around on them silver trays and like, champagne flutes. Imagine that mate! Me mixing with the best of reality. Tell you what though, this really awkward thing happened when I was there. It was this moment of conversation and when it happened right, I remember looking around the room to see if anyone else noticed and no one batted an eyelid. It was started by this one thing this person said.

**Sparx**    Like, what was said like?

**Mark**    We were talking about Woolworths, and I was saying it like it was an intrinsic part of the British high street for years. Going down Balham with your nan on a Saturday. Ladybird books, He-Man toys, Micro Machines, Chad Valley, Pick n Mix and then this woman says this thing. Have a guess what she said?

**Sparx**    I don't know what she said like.

**Mark**    Really, put yourself in the moment right there. Imagine it. Me. Everyone in suits all around. Big plush function. All in dinner jackets holding court in the conversation. Just have a guess. You'll never guess. But guess anyway.

**Sparx**    I can't fucking guess like, what, I keep thinking about the free food and that.

**Mark**    Well, I said, isn't it a shame that all the branches have closed down, and then this women in a power suit, clipped accent and all that, turns around and goes, 'Yeah, isn't it a shame, where will all the chavs buy their Christmas presents now?' Bruv, I couldn't believe it. I was disgusted. Shocked. That's my family bruv.

**Sparx**    Nah. What's wrong with people? It's a joke like. Makes you think though dunnit?

**Mark**    Yeah it does. What?

**Sparx**    Where are they gonna go?

## Scene Five

**Mark** *and* **Sparx** *are smoking outside.*

**Sparx**    E Cigarette? Pussy!

**Mark**    Why are you always drinking milk?

**Sparx**    I'm protein deficient innit? Didn't you know that most people our age are protein deficient like?

**Mark**    No.

**Sparx**    You didn't know that?

**Mark**    No.

**Sparx**    Did no one tell you about the wicked witch who came along and stole all the kids' milk bruv?

**Mark**    Nah.

**Sparx**    No one told you that?

**Mark**    Sounds like one of your YouTube videos bruv.

**Sparx**    That's a fact bruv. Fact.

**Mark**    You, and your little stories mate. You make me laugh.

**Sparx**    The thing about you yeah, is that you believe everything you read in the newspaper innit? Every fucking little thing that you read. Like, 'Oh yeah I believe that'. I'm gonna tell you a newspaper story bruv. Our local paper tried to shame up this girl innit? Made her out to be a tramp. This girl on my estate. Her name was Kelly. She's twenty-one years old. Three babies by three different baby fathers like. But she's cool bruv. No one's shown her the right way to do things innit? She hangs about the estate, she lets some of the man dem chill in her yard and that. She's safe bruv. Case in point, this eighty-nine year old woman on the estate had a birthday, and Kelly put balloons up. Put banners up, got all the local kids dancing and that for this old woman. And she got a shopping trolley and filled it full of vinyls, 70s vinyls for the old lady. Obviously, to me and you, 70s is really old, she was eighty-nine so that was kinda recent. So like, she didn't like those records. I was trying to work out, what kind of records would she like? Maybe like 'Lambeth Walk' or something like that. The point is yeah, that's the kind of thing this girl would do, you know nice things, the old woman had tears in her eyes. Turns out back in the day, she was something like a writer or something, something important. I don't know what happened, but that shopping trolley ended up out the front of Kelly's yard. All the local kids start throwing rubbish in it. Kwik Save No Frills crisp packets. Panda Pop bottles. An old tyre, all that shit. And then some spiteful coked out journo decides to take pictures out the front of her house. Makes her out to be a tramp, bruv. Makes her out to be a scumbag. A young girl like that. THAT'S a fucking newspaper story bruv. She had to quit her job, volunteering in 'Help The Aged' you know.

*They both contemplate the story.* **Sparx** *feels like he has said something deeply philosophical.*

**Mark**    Would you bang her though?

**Sparx**    Na man! . . . She was alright though still.

**Mark** *and* **Sparx** *go back inside.*


**Scene Six**

**Sparx**    Fucking tired. Working so hard tonight. Might have a kip.

**Mark**    There's a couple more centimetres mate, definitely. Definitely.

**Sparx** *falls asleep on the old couch.* **Mark** *starts slowly clicking on the end of a pen, and then starts making rhythms with it. As he gets into it, he gets lost in a trance and builds up into a Bic clicking crescendo.*

**Mark**    Sparxx?. . Mate? . . : Sparxx. . . . Bruv? . . . Sparxx!. . Sparxx! . . . Steve! . . . Steven! . . .

**Sparx**    Fucking hell man! Fucking clicking a fucking pen over and over again and shit.What you doing bruv? I was trying to sleep and that. Don't call me Steven, it's Sparx innit?

**Mark**    Do you want a cup of tea?

**Sparx**    No man.

**Mark**    I know what I was gonna ask you. It was you I was working with the other week right? And you were watching *Scarface* on your phone? Talking about 'being an actor' and that? That was you weren't it?

**Sparx**    Yea, watching *Scarface* innit? I was just saying like, sick film innit? If they needed another Al Pacino. It's mad but . . . it's kinda obvious where they would go.

**Mark**    The reason I'm asking right . . .

**Sparx**   Don't you think about it bruv like? Al Pacino's getting old innit like. Carlito's done. If they needed another Al Pacino . . .

**Mark**   The reason I'm asking right, is cos this funny thing . . .

**Sparx**   Are you thinking about it like? All the places you've worked, all the schools you've been to growing up, all the adults you know. If they needed Al Pacino to be replaced, who the fuck would they come to?

**Mark**   I don't know bruv. . . I

**Sparx**   You don't know about this shit bruv, why you asking me for over and over again?

**Mark**   What I was gonna say, I actually met an actor.

**Sparx**   Recently?

**Mark**   Yeah. Gemma's cousin right. He's just moved to London. I met him at some family barbecue they were having in Croydon. And he's just graduated from some drama school. Originally from up north somewhere. Bristol or something. First time I meet this guy, the first thing he does is start slagging off Croydon.

**Sparx**   Dickhead! Like, who's this prick? Nah bruv!

**Mark**   It's like, he's a bit weird bruv. He has like, thick rimmed glasses a big beard, scruffy hair, weird clothes.

**Sparx**   I know them ones bruv! Was he covered in bare tattoos but he was a pussy?

**Mark**   Yeah!

**Sparx**   I seen that bruv!

**Mark**   You know what? He's actually all right. He's a good guy. We went and watched one of his shows. It was in some sort of weird warehouse place in east London somewhere.

**Sparx**   Weird.

**Mark**   Weird. But I went along with Gemma and I quite enjoyed it. I'd never really been to those sorts of places before. I didn't really know what was going on,

**Sparx**   What was going on?

**Mark**   And I definitely felt out of place. There was no one from London.

**Sparx**    Like no one from ends, innit?

**Mark**    No.

**Sparx**    Weird yeah.

**Mark**    But I liked it, right. I enjoyed it. And afterwards we were having a drink with him in the bar. Bruv, it's so weird yeah. Everyone in there, everyone in there was drinking these weird beers from jam jars and that.

**Sparx**    That's off-key bruv!

**Mark**    But anyway right, he was saying. He runs this club, every week yeah, it's free, and what it is, actors and other performers like comedians stuff, they go down and they do like that improv.

**Sparx**    I know 'bout them tings bro.

**Mark**    You should get involved.

**Sparx**    Me? Some little club and that? Bruv like, imagine me going down there to the club. Imagine that. You know what would happen, innit?

**Mark**    No.

**Sparx**    Me just rolling up to their little thing. Is that fair? Obviously, you know what's gonna happen innit?

**Mark**    Not really, not until you go.

**Sparx**    I'll fucking shut it down man! I know about them acting things like. I used to go to this boys' school everyone there was banging out rugby, football, athletics all them things bruv. And it's like I couldn't get involved . . . I was born with a bad heart.

**Mark**    Really?

**Sparx**    Yeah bruv really like. Obviously you look at me and think 'semi pro footballer?' Rugby and that? Nah bruv. Nah, like. I couldn't get involved. I had to stick out, I had to make my own lane. So I told jokes that make people laugh and that. I'd swear at the teachers, take my trousers down, jump on the table and get my dick out. All that shit, bruv. In drama, it gave me the confidence everyone was watching and laughing, watching for what I would do next. I remember us doing impros . . . I started reading scripts, monologues and that doing all these scenes bruv. And then the drama teacher said, he said there was gonna be this drama club on Wednesday, and I thought 'a drama club?' That's ME! That's gonna be my thing. I knew it there and then: that's me. I couldn't wait for that Wednesday man. I even told my mum about it.

**Mark**    Yeah?

**Sparx**    She said it was 'gay' but anyway I fucking told her. I remember on that Wednesday in maths, it was all coming at me, I couldn't even compute it bruv. Remember slamming my books down, going down the corridor, walking into that classroom, forgot my books in the classroom. I walked in there . . . it's like . . . There was no one there, I was just one man up.

**Mark**    So, what happened?

**Sparx**    Drama teacher like, just carried that club on. One on one, week after week. We did characterizations we did improvisations, monologues, duologues, scenes. We put on some plays and that. Obviously, like, after two years he left the school. I stopped doing it and that. That's when I realised, it's just a fucking waste of time waste of time and that. No point. Bullshit.

**Mark**    So let me get this straight, so when you were at school, you did drama?

**Sparx**    Yeah man.

**Mark**    *You* were a pussy?

**Sparx**    I'll still knock you out man!

**Mark**    I'm only messing man. But in all seriousness, why don't you do it now? You're working, earning.

**Sparx**    Working? We're not even getting fucking paid man. And you got all these drama school auditions. There's bare nepotism in that game. Bruv, they help and they scratch each-others' backs and that. 'Internships' all that shit bruv.

**Mark**    What is an internship?

**Sparx**    Something that posh people do man.

**Mark**    Shame, bruv. Real shame. My dad always said 'It's good to have hobbies.' Something creative. Acting, painting. I wish I had a talent like that.

**'Paul Gascoigne'** *Spoken Word Interlude*

**Mark**
As I kid, I idolised Paul Gascoigne
Even when the nation watched him fall
With a ball at his feet, there weren't many better
The complete player he had it all
On playgrounds and in parks, I tried to mimic his tricks,
Cruyff turns, defence splitting passes and pin-point free kicks
He lit fires of excitement like beacons in bellies
From small boys to fully grown men we watched tellies and he gave
    us hope
He held boredom by the throat
And just like us, he was one of your own
He played in parks and in boys' clubs
And despite being a pro he drank larger from the glass
On the playground and in PE, he was the one we wanted to be
He set the template for what could be achieved
I must have been fifteen when I stopped dreaming
I was still playing, but I barely made the bench on my own team
Under fifteen's Sunday league
Paul Gascoigne, was a freak.
Blessed with diamond-like properties at his feet he was one in a million
And I was in one in the nine hundred and ninety-nine thousand that
    weren't brilliant
My dad told me that, so did my teachers and so did my mates
But not before I'd already told myself
Them saying it only validated my mind-state
Come sixteen I wanted to leave school, get a job, and one day get
    married have kids.
Have holidays to Florida and a house with a mortgage.
And if I could afford it, a nice car.
I'd play golf or snooker with my mates on the weekend
And afterwards sink a couple of jars,
Then return home, and spend the evening with the wife and kids
Watching reality TV shows, because that's reality right?
I don't want be a Paul Gascoigne, or any celebrity,
Because I can't be.
I'm nine hundred and ninety-nine thousand people combined,
And if I find a wannabe Paul Gascoigne, I'll wish him the best of luck
But to be honest, he's better off getting a real job
Just like the rest of us.

**Sparx**   Hobbies bruv? You could start anything anytime you wanted. You're extra bruv. You go IN. So fucking extra. Man like you, goes to work every day. You're the type of guy that checks holes in fences. Over and over a – fucking – gen. You're that dude who checks charts to see who came on time. Who came in late. Grassing on man. You're clever clogs bruv. You're fucking jobsworth innit? You can do anything you want innit.

**Mark**   What me?

**Sparx**   Yeah.

**Mark**   Hardly mate. Tell you what, before I started here, I was unemployed for two years mate. Signing on the whole time.

**Sparx**   You?

**Mark**   Yeah.

**Sparx**   Mister clever clogs?

**Mark**   Yeah. 'Mister clever clogs'. I remember, I tried everything. I applied for everything. Online every day. Going up and down the high streets giving in CVs. Filling in endless job application forms. I find those things really hard bruv. I'm dyslexic. I got turned down for Tesco's, Sainsbury's, JD Sports, Costa Coffee, Superdrug, call centres, data admin, clerical admin, traffic warden. I remember I got turned down for Tie Rack.

**Sparx**   Tie Rack?

**Mark**   Tie Rack! That was the only one that I had an interview for right. And I remember it, because I proper psyched myself up for it. During the interview I got completely bamboozled. Gobsmacked. Couldn't anything. Person interviewing me right, goes 'MARK, tell us why you want to work at Tie Rack?'

**Sparx**   Bruv like. Why did you wanna work at Tie Rack?

**Mark**   Bruv I didn't care, I just wanted a flipping job. I would've gone down the sewers if they sent me. It didn't matter. I was desperate. I would've done anything, and I thought that was obvious. I couldn't answer the question. I couldn't say nothing. Words wouldn't come out. Bruv, the whole two years, Gemma was supporting both of us. On her receptionist wages. Mate there is no way on planet Earth I want to go back to filling in those fucking job seekers' diaries.

**Sparx**   No way . . . You, like.

**Mark**   Me.

**Sparx**   Went through all that?

**Mark**    Yeah.

**Sparx**    Fucking mad. Making me think like. We both went through all that shit bruv, like.

**Mark**    Yeah.

**Sparx**    Now we're fucking here, going through the same fucking shit.

**Mark**    Yeah.

**Sparx**    Mad bruv.

**Mark**    Careful there. That's starting to sound like union talk mate.

**Sparx**    Nah man. Not banging on about all this fucking union shit. Just saying like. Going through the same shit.

**Mark**    Seriously though, I know that's not your cup of tea, all that stuff. Whilst we're working here together like, I've got your back bruv.

**Sparx**    Have ya?

**Mark**    Yeah.

**Sparx**    Cool man.

**Mark**    And you got mine? We could make our own little union.

**Sparx**    Mark & Sparx yeah?

**Mark**    We look after each other.

**Sparx**    Yeah?

**Mark**    Yeah.

**Sparx**    Do you want a tea like?

**Mark**    Yeah.

*Phone rings.*

**Mark**    It's Wayne! Hello Wayne! . . . Not too bad.

**Sparx**    Why's Wayne calling you like? Bruv ask him about a cash advance or something.

**Mark**    Yeah all good. Yeah, yeah.

**Sparx**    Maybe he's gonna ask you about 'Friday drinks' and that.

**Mark**   Yeah, another twenty minutes or so and we'll do the final round. All quiet mate, nothing to report. Yeah I got a minute, yeah. Oh, right. Yeah. No, he didn't say nothing.

**Sparx**   So bait.

**Mark**   Right. Hold on. Nothing? Nothing at all? All right. One of them, I understand. Look Wayne, I'm probably gonna have to sort something else out. Can I put your name down . . . You can't do that? All right. No, I understand. All right. Cheers, bruv. You too. Alright mate. Thanks.

**Sparx**   What's going on? What's he saying? Wayne and that like. What's he saying? MARK. . . . . . . . . . .MARK. . . . . . . . . . . . . MARK!

**Mark**   I've got no shifts next week.

**Sparx**   Is it?

**Mark**   And none for the foreseeable future. You've got thirty-seven and a half hours next week

**Sparx**   Have I?

**Mark**   And you've known since last Tuesday.

**Sparx**   Bruv you must be pissed. Like, really fucking pissed. I know what you're thinking. I know EXACTLY what. Who is gonna look after this place? I am! I'm gonna do those charts bruv, over and over again. Man's gonna sweep the floor. I'll even search out here for the fucking holes bruv! Check the holes out four times a shift. Probably be like two times innit like? Cos my two times is like your four times. Bruv I'm here innit like? Don't worry about that man. I'm looking after this place innit. We cool like? It's 'Mark & Sparx' and that like. You said that. Mark? I couldn't have done anything.

**Sparx** *picks up* **Mark***'s ruler.*

Can I keep that?. . . . . . .

**Sparx** *looks out of the window at the hole.*

**Sparx**   I think it's getting bigger man. . . . . . . .

**Mark** *walks out.*

**Sparx**   Good luck.

   **'No Milk For The Foxes'** *Final Rap*

   *Verse 1 –* **Sparx**

They don't know how it is they don't know how we live
they don't know how we love they don't know how we give
they say we're shit, they think we ain't shit
that we don't earn shit but we ain't got the chance to learn shit
they call us feckless but we ain't the people with all the money acting
    reckless
change the goalposts constantly just to test us
the only time they came on to our estates, is when they came to
    arrest us
they say we're lacking aspiration but most people in poverty,
are working hard, blood, tears, perspiration
they made their money sitting on their arse
we made our money making things but that's a thing of the past
RIP the working class they're the haves
but we're not the have-nots, we're the chavs
and our humanity been lost

*Chorus*

They know the value of nothing
sure, yet they know just what the cost is
don't know what the loss is
No more milk for the foxes
They know the value of nothing
sure, yet sure they know just what the cost is
don't know what the loss is
No more milk for the foxes

*Verse 2 –* **Mark**

Walk like I'm in a bathtub
having run up a bar tab for ten lads on a big stag
arms given up like retired jazz hands
legs weighed down with inertia, neck feigning a scratch
all of this to earn a scratch and the right to reside in a postcode in the
    smoke
chose that path and I ran, trying to make that train in the rain
Why do I do this, I say
it's 7.45 am and the weekend is four days away
promo girls and boys greet me with a TV smile
smile they say and I take that free product and head on my way
cocky pricks in bibs with clipboards have the gall to call me 'fella'
    and 'geezer'

trying to get me to donate to a place that's worlds away
minus the commission and glossy ad-campaigns
not today mate, out my way bruv, I'm running late
start picking up my pace
ducking umbrellas in my face
all these shops just look the same
another chain with a different name
selling that brand on the cup
that's drunk on the train
de-ja-vu this street scene is on loop
like getting that letter from a creditor
stating that my credit-card payment is overdue
can't work out what to do
I lack the skill-set
numbers get muddled in my brain
get in trouble when I have my review
can't work out what to do
I've got no value and
this job is destroying my attitude
finally I arrive outside
my journey's come to an end
my work day's about to begin
in my chair I sink, eyes fixed on the screen
blood pumping sugar and caffeine
this is what I do
this is what I do

*Chorus*

They know the value of nothing
sure, yet they know just what the cost is
don't know what the loss is
No more milk for the foxes
They know the value of nothing
sure, yet sure they know just what the cost is
don't know what the loss is
No more milk for the foxes

*End.*

# DenMarked

Conrad Murray

*DenMarked* was first performed at Battersea Arts Centre on 12 November 2015.

Recordings of some of the tracks for this performance are available on YouTube, Apple Music, Spotify and SoundCloud.

This is a one-person show, performed as a monologue with musical/rap interludes. Conrad (originally played by Conrad Murray) is the only character.

**Creative Team**

| | |
|---|---|
| *Director* | Ria Parry/Laura O'Keefe |
| *Dramaturgical Advisor* | Emma Rice |
| *Lighting Designer* | Mitch Hargreaves |
| *Producer* | Liz Moreton |
| *Script Development* | Warren Fitzgerald |
| *Sound Designer* | Keir Vine |

**Preshow**

**Conrad** *plays the guitar on stage as the audience walk in and take their seats.* **Conrad** *speaks all dialogue and performs all musical numbers.*

## 1. Interview

Sitting on a hot bus full of commuters, my suit feeling a little bit too tight. My hair is slick and coiffed. I can't wear my trademark New Era cap with this get up, it wouldn't work.

My bag is heavy with books for last minute cramming, fuck knows what kind of material I expect to be learning or reminding myself of on a forty-minute bus journey.

IEPs. I . . . E . . . Ps. Individual Education Plans, individual education plans . . . Must remember to mention that I've been a tutor.

So I arrive, and I'm thirty minutes early. Do I go in? They might think that I'm creepy or over eager. But if I go wandering, I might be late. I know me. I know me.

Ok, text Barry, brother, always knows. He says going in is ok. It's ok! I'll grab a coffee from the cafe next door, and then I'll go in.

So, I've got this takeaway coffee, and I'm trying to figure out how to get in this door. It won't open. I'm pushing, yet it won't open!! Ok. Calm down. Style it out. Must be another door. I walk around, but the doors are locked and gated. What am I gonna do?

I see a student! She tells me she will show me to reception. So, she walks me back towards the original door I couldn't get through, only to reveal a doorbell blatantly in view. Why hadn't I seen this shit before?! Had they seen me trying in vain now walking back with this student looking like a knob? Who the fuck knows? Anyway, I speak to the woman on the intercom, who has a very posh accent, and I get let in.

I meet the woman, the posh one, and within one minute of speaking to me, she has taken all my details, taken my photo, and created a rather nifty photo ID card.

I start feeling very present. Suddenly everything I'm wearing feels scruffy and tight, and I'm regretting this coffee cup in my hand. This makes me look extremely rude, I think to myself. What have I done? Should I hide it?

I start convincing myself that I'm not going to get this job because of this coffee cup. They are going to know exactly what kind of lowlife I am all because of this cardboard coffee cup. I don't deserve to be here. I'm a piece of shit. How can the agency not have seen this? How? Why am I here? What the fuck am I thinking? I can't talk properly, I have bad handwriting, I haven't read *King Lear*, and I call myself a drama teacher?!

*What have you, my good friends, deserved at the hands of fortune that she sends you to prison hither?*

Is that *Hamlet* or *Lear*? Fuck, I can't remember!

*Prison my lord . . . We think not so.*

*To me it is a prison.*

And what happens when they see this cardboard cup of coffee? I'm going to look like a fraud! They are going to know that I am a blagger! I grew up on a council estate and I'm here in this school. A fuck up like me teaching their kids? I don't deserve the opportunity to be around these kids.

There's a girl with her mother to my left, being expelled. Even this bad kid is better than me. She talks better, more articulate, more eloquent.

I've got to look professional and not look at them. The mother is giving the daughter a good talking to. I gotta stop listening in on their conversation.

Where the fuck is this woman who I'm supposed to be meeting? I got here fifteen minutes early, and now it's 10.28! The agency said that our meeting was at 10.30! I need her to come, see me for the piece of shit that I am, say thanks for the opportunity for meeting her, and leave.

Fuck!

I'm so hot and my belly is relaxing more and more into this jacket, making it tighter, making me hotter and more uncomfortable. Great!

*Why then 'tis none to you. For there is nothing either good or bad, but thinking makes it so . . .*

I need to mention Shakespeare, IEPs and get the fuck out of here. I look like a knob, and I sound like one.

I should of just worn my New Era cap and been done with it. Let them see the real me. The piece of shit. The animal. The idiot. The crook.

*Denmark's a prison.*

*Then the world is one.*

## 2. On the Buses

'Conrad don't be so stupid!'

'What's your mum's real job?'

Everyone was laughing at me.

My mum *did* drive a bus.

A double-decker bus!

But for some reason, my teacher didn't believe me.

They were so jealous.

Some days she would let me miss days off of school to ride with her.

I felt so proud. My mum was in control of the whole bus.

They gave *her* all the money.

She used to do impressions of the customers to make me laugh.

'You bloody woman!' [silly accent]

'Women shouldn't drive buses!'

'Five minutes late!'

She drove a bus. Probably one of the most important people. Taking the old ladies where they need to go.

'Shouldn't you be at school young man?'

'No. . . .'

Taking all the clever people to their jobs and to uni.

My mum was in charge.

Most of the time I'd fall asleep on the journey, thinking about how lucky we were.


## 3. Remember Me?

The last time I saw my dad before our eighteen-year hiatus he asked me to remember. 'Remember.'

And he smiled.

It was weird because it wasn't just him that he wanted me to remember, but he wanted me to remember my mum and what she was like, and what he put up with.

Why he broke her nose.

Why he slammed her hands in doors and covered her in bruises.

*Adieu, Adieu, Adieu. Remember me!*

My earliest memory of my parents ended with my dad choking my mum. He choked her until blood came out of her eyes and mouth.

It was the day of the dad of my dad's funeral. So technically my grandad. But I had never met him as he lived in India.

It was pitch black.

The room was hot and sweaty.

And stinky. A weird smell. A strange disgusting smell. It was filled with grunts and moans.

'Mum, Can I have a glass of water?'

'Get it yourself!'

I was about four years old.

I knew something weird was happening.

The door flings open.

The light blazes through the darkness.

'Dad! Can YOU get me a glass of water?'

I hear trousers being frantically pulled up. Two adults fumbling around in the dark. One of them, a strange man.

Heavy breathing.

'*Fuck fuck fuck!*'

A belt buckle hastily fastened, the metal clasp constantly missing the hole.

My mum is already grizzling and crying.

Why is she crying?

My dad is in his railway uniform, dark blue, wearing a satchel, which he throws to the ground. He calmly walks into the kitchen and makes me a glass of water. He walks in, passes it to me shouts 'Whore!' and immediately punches the strange man so hard that his head hits the ceiling.

My mum is screaming at me to go to bed. It's funny. . . I'm not allowed to watch this part.

My dad punches the man again, who isn't fighting back. There is blood streaming out of his nose. He then throws the man out of the window. We lived on the second floor.

He then started choking my mother.

'Can you see what your fucking mother has done to me? Don't fucking forget this.'

*Yea from the table of my memory*
*I'll wipe away all trivial fond records*
*All saws of books, all forms, all pressures past*
*. That youth and observation copied there*
*And thy commandment all alone shall live*
*Within the book and volume of my brain.*

The last time I saw my dad was fleetingly in a court room, and in those few seconds he said, 'Conny. Remember? Remember that glass of water?'

*Remember me. Adieu. Adieu.*

## 4. No Books (*sung (italics), rapped*)

*We never had no books in our house*
*We only had some crooks in our house*
*My family*
*Only thing to me*
*We never had no hope in the yard*
*I spent my evenings talking to God*
*Lord can't you see*
*My family*

I never had deference for my own mum
'Cos she was so young
A runaway teen
It's funny cos I knew her before she was eighteen
I was five years old

Sitting on my own in the flat in the cold
Writing on walls
Pissing on floors
I remember opening drawers
And throwing shit about
And putting old medicines in my little brother's mouth
He nearly died
Sitting in the hospital
Watching my mum cry
Yet we were alone on the next night
Playing with matches and starting fires

*We never had no books in our house*
*We only had some crooks in our house*
*My family*
*Only thing to me*
*We never had no hope in the yard*
*I spent my evenings talking to God*
*Lord can't you see*
*My family. . . .*

Thinking about the day
When Paki bashing was all the rage
I watched my dad come home
His head split open
He was in pain
I was so confused
My mum looked at me and said,
'This could be you!'
And from that day
I knew
What I would have to do
Cover my face
Cover my shame
Cover my skin and protect my name.
I hated my dad for being brown
He was to blame
I used to pray to be white
Wanted to be right
Watched my dad's head pissing with blood that night

*We never had no books in our house*
*We only had some crooks in our house*
*My family*

*Only thing to me*
*We never had no hope in the yard*
*I spent my evenings talking to God*
*Lord can't you see*
*My family . . . .*
*My family*
*My family*
*My family*


## 5. Estates

Ivy bridge estate.
Laburnham estate.
Eastfields estate.
My estates.

I don't live on an estate anymore, but my experiences on them continues to shape the way in which I think about the world outside. Like the rappers who continue to talk about the ghetto experience long after they have moved on out and into their cribs.

It's a life-long estate of mind.

There was a Gateways on our estate, and when I was around five or six, me and Barry were running around. Me, my bro, my mum and my dad. And I remember seeing some kids from school with their families, and I just wanted to hide.

I felt dread and embarrassment.

I don't think I even knew the other kids' names. But somehow, I was already ashamed to be seen with my dad. I knew there was some sort of stigma attached to being seen with him. I don't know why.

The fact that he was drunk everyday?

That he had a strange accent and funny way of talking?

I don't know.

But then I guess, everyone is ashamed of their parents, aren't they?


## 6. Dad

*To sleep . . . To sleep perchance to dream.*
*Ay. There's the rub.*

*For in that sleep of death*
*What dreams may come . . .*

I've always had the same dream ever since I was a kid. The only thing that has changed is that I get older in the dream. Like, when I was five, I was five in the dream, and then when I was ten and so on. It always feels completely real. I dream that I'm in prison, and throughout the whole night I am anxious and confused as to why I am in this cell. I wake up in a sweat. Strangely, the experience has lost its terror as I wake, and it has now become this regular feature of my life. I used to feel really, really scared, but now, it's just like . . . part of me.

When I'm out shopping, or amongst people I'm working with, I've always had this paranoia, that they somehow know about the dream. That whatever I'm doing isn't proper, that I'm either going to steal, or that I shouldn't actually be doing what I'm doing and that somehow I've tricked my way in. After all it's only a matter of time before I'm really going to end up in prison, right?

There have been times when my fate has felt so inescapable, that I've just thought 'fuck it', and kind of gone along with the inevitable, made problems for myself. It's almost as if I just wanted to get the prison part of my life over and done with.

There's stockings on the wall, coca-cola can red with brilliant white trimmings at the top, filled with presents. Mum's crying on the phone. She's been crying all night. I've heard her cry many times before, but this is different.

You went out last night and didn't come back, Dad.

It's Christmas day.

In my stocking I get a Transformers wallet.

'Robots in disguise!'

It has this hologram effect where you move it left to right, and the transformer on it moves left and right. It seems like magic to me.

Me and Barry get the same presents. Exactly the same. I don't know if he remembers the wallets, but I do know that he remembers *that* Christmas.

We both get chemistry sets which have hard-to-follow instructions, so we just end up mashing all the chemicals together and the box and all the test tubes explode.

It was a madness.

We were five years old.

There's people in the house and everyone's talking in hushed tones about you. Nan and Grandad, and Uncle A and Darren are round. Mum's angry and sobbing. I'm sad that you're not here. I don't think anyone else is to be honest with you, Dad. Everyone just seems really concerned about Mum. And so I feel guilty for wishing you were here.

Everyone's talking at once now and I keep hearing parts of a story.

'Smashed a glass everywhere. . . . Face totally torn up. . . . Sliced up. . . . He might die. . . . Dunno Deb. . . . It's serious. . . . Dunno how long it's gonna be . . .'

Parts of a story.

I'm scared, a little confused. It seems something's happened to you.

But at the same time I'm totally mesmerized by the drama I'm creating with some of my other presents. He-Man's bashing Skeletor's head in whilst Orko cheers him on.

Man, He-Man was SICK!

But now I'm desperate to know where you are. It's been so long since I've seen you. A whole day! And that's like forever, right? And I keep asking Mum and she tries to ignore me, but I keep going on and on and on and on. And then she just blurts it out. She just comes out with it: 'He's in prison. He has done something really bad to this man and he is probably gonna be there for a long time, the selfish bastard, leaving me with no money coming in, what am I going to do eh?'

And thinking about it now. There was no comforting from Mum. She was just concerned for herself really.

And what did you leave *me* with, Dad? A big inheritance that's what. And that inheritance is the dream, the dream about being locked up and that sense of inevitability. Inevitability that the dream will soon come true.

*O God, I could be bounded in a nutshell and count myself a king of infinite space, were it not that I have bad dreams.*

*Which dreams indeed are ambition. For the very substance of the ambitious is merely the shadow of a dream.*

## 7. Lost Father Lost

I loved going over Tooting Bec Common, with my grandad and nan, fishing. We would sit there for hours with a bag of sweets, catching fish, and then throwing them back.

The maggots always smelled so bad.

I was fascinated by my grandad. He spent thirty years working on the post, making it to a PHG. Postman Higher Grade. As we sat there by the pond, in a spot that we always sat in, he would talk about the old days.

'Your Nan would take the telegram boys in cakes and sweets. They were young lads, rough around the edges. I kept 'em in shape, but we had fun too. Playing table tennis and going bowing. I was like a father figure to those lads.'

Father figure. Hmmm. Like a lot of my mates, my grandad was always a bit of a father figure to me. My dad was too pissed up or passed out to teach me about the world. So it was up to my grandad to teach me the ways of the wide world. Trouble was, he was from the old world, even though he wasn't old. He never went out to the pub, went home every night to my nan, ate tea, shaved, walked the dog and went to bed at the same time every night.

He would tell me about the postal strike in 1971, and how he had to find ways to top up his pay, as they were all on benefits at the time. He was a paid-up member of the Labour Party and had been his whole life. This meant he would only read *The Mirror*, and would complain that my mum read *The Sun*.

If I asked him about his childhood, he was always a bit vague, but honest.

'You know me, Con. I'm not a clever man. I like to buy all my gear and read me old books. Never went to school and all that. That's not for people like us. I'm not bitter. There are people like us, and there are people like them. You work hard, you live a good life.'

Him and my nan still lived in his family home, which his mum had lived in since before the war. He said they hadn't been lucky in getting one of the new post war council houses. Their place had no bathroom whatsoever, gas pipes everywhere, and an old 'leccy meter. They did have electricity, and he was training to become an electrician. My grandad had fitted it all himself until . . .

'Got scared of electric Conny. Didn't wanna do that anymore.'

He was dead against ownership of houses, and when their house in what used to be derided Balham, gateway to the south, was offered for them to buy at low rate. He refused.

'You can't just sell off the houses Conny. Where are people gonna live? The government should look after houses so that there are homes always there. You don't want to take it back to the old days do ya? We are lucky to have the place we have.'

Everyone said their house was haunted. That there was this weird feeling in the house. I hated it when they spoke about it. Creepy.

My grandad would talk about all sorts of issues in his life, but wouldn't go into any detail. His childhood was a mystery. Until my nan told me, 'Your grandad came home from school when he was twelve and found his dad with his head in his oven. He was having doo daas with the lady next door, dirty bugger, and was scared that the whole street would find out. So he took his own life in the cooker, to be found by Tone when he came home from school. It was a nasty shock.'

I have asked my grandad about his dad.

'I don't want to talk about him. You don't talk about them days.'

What with my grandad not really knowing his father, my dad leaving India as a teenager and not knowing his for long, and me not knowing my dad for years, I often wonder how I will eventually desert my children? *If* I have 'em.

> *Your father lost a father,*
> *That father lost, lost his, and the survivor bound*
> *In filial obligation for some term*
> *To do obsequious sorrow. But to persevere*
> *In obstinate condolement is a course*
> *Of impious stubbornness. 'Tis unmanly grief.*

## 8. I Sang

The first time that I sang at school, was the first time I ever received a compliment from anyone.

I had been singing for years. Ever since I was around five. My teacher actually called up my parents, to tell them that she thought that I was gifted, as I could naturally pitch, find harmonies, and had an inherent timing ability. I used to listen to records for hours, copying all the sounds and vocals.

*Sings.*

> *You're the cutest lover doll*
> *That I ever did ever did see*
> *Let me tell you lover doll*
> *You were meant, just meant for me*
> *From the first time that I saw you*
> *How I fell for your girly charms*
> *Lover doll I'm crazy for you*
> *Let me rock you in my arms . . .*

I had even learned melodies and bass notes on a one-stringed guitar that we had.

Because of this, Mum decided that I *didn't* need lessons, which my teacher had advised, as I had natural talent. So, Barry got lessons instead. Years later I was able to teach *him* guitar.

Anyway, I had won a singing contest and told my teacher and she suggested that I sing to the class.

I was really nervous, as Danny Evans and Jamal Waters were in. Jamal had spat in my hair three times this week as it was Black history month, and this was his form of reparations.

I took a deep breath and sang my winning song, which had won my family a caravan holiday at Haven.

The class went deadly silent.

I had every reason to expect the usual, my bag turned over, phlegm in my books, oranges squashed into my jacket, when the world shook – as I finished, I got an applause. A *big* one.

Danny Evans actually came over and said, 'That was good Con', when everyone had left.

Didn't even call me Condom.

Swear down I was left alone. For about a week.

## 9. Julie

I spent so long looking for you online. I tried Facebook, Twitter and even MySpace. Nothing came up. I wanted to tell you you're one of the most special people I've ever known. You listened. And you were really tall. Or maybe I was just really small.

I kept typing your name in. Julie. Julie Morro. Nothing came up. But you might have changed your name, got married, or . . .

Do you remember when you used to take me out for burgers and milkshakes, and you let me order anything I wanted? And I was like, 'REALLY?' and you smiled and said, 'Of course.' So I ordered a Big Mac meal, chicken nuggets, a sundae, two apple pies and a large chocolate milkshake.

Remember we used to talk about anything? As well as all the shit at home, you'd let me go on about my dreams and ambitions.

> . . . *the very substance of the ambitious is merely the shadow of a dream.*

But you listened. I told you about my singing, and how I'd listen to records for hours, learning all the words.

I couldn't believe it at first, that they let me miss days off of school to spend time with you. In fact, they *made* me miss days off of school to spend time with you.

You listened. Made me feel human when I told you that I got beat up at school, then went home and got beat up some more.

If I ever talked about you at home, all I'd hear was, 'She's from the social, she's meddling, she don't care about you.' But I knew different. I knew you cared. You helped me stop getting detentions by signing my homework diary as mum refused. She said I'd be grounded and sent to bed early if I ever asked her again.

There was one time though when I did feel you let me down. I was just tucking into my second apple pie when you asked me whether there had been, 'Any incidents at home?' I said 'No, not really.' You said, 'It's ok Conrad, you can tell me. That's what I'm here for.'

So I just told you I'd been hit a few times and dad pushed me into the bushes on Monday.

I couldn't believe it when you said that you had to let my parents know what I'd told you. It was the law.

When we got to my house, you told my parents that you had to put it into a report. They were all understanding, laughing and smiles. That was until you left, then it was, 'What the fuck did you tell Julie? We won't be able to get rid of her now.' And I'd get more beats, for telling about the beats.

At school Mr Hillman, ten foot tall, looked like a zombie, never blinked, sent me out the class for a minute, whilst he oh so helpfully told my peers that I was abused at home, and that I had a social worker. Oh, this was *so* helpful.

I went back into the classroom, with whispers all around me of 'Haha Condom gets beats!'

('Haha Condom'.)

I never ever blamed you for this. You were always good to me. You had to say something, right?

It was the law.

And you were so tall.

Or was I just really small?

## 10. Psychiatrist

> *I will be brief: your noble son is mad.*
> *Mad call I it, for, to define true madness,*
> *What is 't but to be nothing else but mad?*

So, I went to the Psychiatrist, Dr Bryn Williams, as my parents tried to blame me for some of the incidents at home. And I told him:

'My parents give me beats all the time.'

And he's like, 'Yes, and do you touch yourself?'

'When we go on holiday, they make me sleep on the kitchen floor in the caravan because I still wet the bed.'

'Yes, but do you find that you touch yourself often?'

'The fucking fridge freezer buzzes in my face all night as I shiver on the shiny washable lino.'

And the shrink's like, 'And what do you think of your penis?'

I'm twelve. And my hips are bruised in the morning by the hard floor and my skin stings from piss-soaked sores.

'Yes,' goes Dr Williams, 'Yes, but what do you think about your penis?'

And I'm thinking: what the FUCK has this got to do with my penis?? This is supposed to help me, innit?

## 11. Hiding (*rapped and sung*)

I felt hated
alienated
a grey kid
not black or white
I was wrong not right

*I was hiding*
*I was hiding*
*we were shook*

we left behind our benefit books
couldn't go back there
because we were too scared
*we were hiding*
*hiding*

Picture the scene
Picture a little me
writhing in agony
my grandma in a blood-soaked sari
my dad crying on the floor saying sorry
everybody scared saying 'Don't worry'
My dad had stabbed me in the head
I spent the whole night
thinking I would wake up dead
the whole pillow was stained red
in took two grown men to pull the blunt instrument out
everybody stared to shout
blood started to piss
an old Indian lady giving me a kiss
a fork deep into my temple
created this tempest
a foreign instrument unto me imparted
henceforth from this family foreign
I'll be departed

*I was hiding*
*We were hiding*

I felt hated
alienated
a grey kid

not black or white
I was wrong not right
*I was hiding*
*I was hiding*
we were shook
we left behind our benefit books
couldn't go back there
because we were too scared
*we were hiding*
*we were hiding*

Although times were tough
and we had a few hurdles
I remember me and Barry playing Ninja Turtles
but like the ghost at the feast
we couldn't get away from the beast

He turned up when Barry was nine
it was his birthday
he fucked it up the worst way

'Happy Birthday son'
Then he kicked him up some
then he started fucking up my mum
But, she fought back with her bus cash tray
he was looking right at me
*'Alas poor father, I knew thee well'*
He was drunk pissed
now here hung those lips
as an infant mewling, I had oft kissed

I felt hated
alienated
a grey kid
not black or white
I was wrong not right
*I was hiding*
*I was hiding*
we were shook
we left behind our benefit books
couldn't go back there
because we were too scared
*we were hiding*
*hiding*

## 12. Dawn

There was a girl on the estate who everyone used to cuss. They called her simple. I used to hang around with her at a spot called Pains Close.

She had braces, and blonde really straight lank hair. Her make-up was overdone, and she obviously thought that an abundance of make-up on her face made her look like a grown up. But it was kinda messy and it looked like it was done by a kid. Well, she was a kid.

> *I have heard of your paintings too, well enough*
> *God has given you one face and you make yourselves another.*
> *You jig and amble, and you lisp,*
> *You nickname God's creatures and you make your wantonness your*
> *ignorance.*

She always wore tracksuits, and she was skinny. She used to get off with all the boys, and everyone said that she had had sex in the graveyard.

For some reason she took a liking to me, and one summer, we hung around every day. I was a bit embarrassed, because other people I knew on the estate tried cussed me off, saying I was 'hanging round with a slag'.

I would just be like 'No, she follows me around, dirty bitch'. And sometimes I'd say it in front of her. But she didn't seem to mind, and just waited for them to go away and we would ride bikes or hang around the park.

The truth is, that even though I had seen her make out with loads of other boys, and everyone cussed her, I did like her, whatever that meant.

One time, she asked me to sit in a tree with her, I was scared about this because one: I would have to climb (it wasn't that high though), and two: because no one was around. It was like eight-thirty, still light in the summer, but there was that strange breeze and eerie feeling you get as the sun is beginning to go down. It was like a memory was being made as it was happening.

'Close your eyes', she said. My heart was pounding, because of the climb, I could feel it in my mouth. I thought I was going to puke.

She said, 'Open them', and as I did I could see her big head in front of mine, and she kissed me on the lips.

I still remember the feel of her braces.

I just felt immediately angry. And sick. I jumped down from the tree, and never said anything. I could hear her saying 'Conrad' as I scurried off.

I never spoke to her again. Every day I could see her sitting on the bench out the back, waiting for me to come out. I just stayed in bed confused. She even knocked on my door. My mum said I was ill.

It was a shame, because no one liked her, and she was kinda abused by the other boys. She went to a special needs school. I think she was quite vulnerable. People called her a hoe and a sket, and although I liked her, I wasn't really ready for sexual contact.

I felt really guilty, but I couldn't handle these kind of feelings at the time. I'm not sure I've ever been able to deal with them properly.

## 13. Mum

*Come come and sit you down. You shall not budge.*
*You go not till I set you up a glass*
*Where you may see the inmost part of you.*

So, you make a huge song and dance about not letting us play out front. But eventually you let us. So me and Barry see Michael and Tenisha, your best friend Barbara's kids, playing near the school gates. So me and Barry wander down. It's so close to our house on the estate this school. That's why you make us go there. 'Cos it's so close. No matter that I hate it, that I think it's fucking shit. It's easy to convince Michael and Tenisha the same thing. Easy to make them see that this school owes us some basketballs for ruining my life.

So we're pulling apart the doors of the gym and jamming in bits of wood to get leverage when I start to feel sick, feel like I've gone too far, feel like I'm proving you right about what a fuck up I truly was. A good for nothing who would end up in prison.

To me *this* is a prison.

*For there is nothing either good or bad but thinking makes it so.*
*To me it is a prison.*

'Put it down lads.' I nearly shit my pants as I turn around and see two police officers slamming Michael and Tenisha up against the wall, twisting their arms up behind their backs and making them cry.

And we're all frogmarched across the estate in front of everyone. All the other kids shouting, jeering, laughing. And I'm so shamed up. It's Barry's birthday barbeque – he's twelve – so the whole family's round enjoying the drama of seeing us carted off by the feds.

It's my first time being arrested. A big moment, I think. The first of many.

And there's you, Mum, shaking your head. And smiling. Smiling. And your voice echoes down the estate after me.

'You're just like your father. He's just like his father.'

And I feel myself transforming. 'Robots in disguise!' Confirming, conforming, becoming, the piece of shit you say I am. At first it's hand and glove, but then with the fear and the shame I realise it's more like a Nintendo DS cartridge into a Gameboy.

Kind of the same, you know, they look the same, but it doesn't properly fit, that combination doesn't work and potentially it's breaking that shit.

> *O wonderful son that can so 'stonish a mother!*

'You're just like your father. He's just like his father.'

> *I will speak daggers to her, but use none*
> *My tongue and soul in this be hypocrites.*

> *Come come and sit you down. You shall not budge.*
> *You go not till I set you up a glass*
> *Where you may see the inmost part of you.*

## 14. Julie Part 2

I had the dream again, that I end up in prison. That I was just like him.

I had done something horrible. Something evil. And I was paying the price.

A dream is in itself a shadow.

Sometimes he would be in the dreams, like a being from another world.

Reminding me that I am him, and he's me. A psycho, an alcoholic and a bum.

Is this what I am destined to be?

Perhaps there's a divinity that shapes our ends?

But I'm due a new start.

Julie thinks that I can sing, and that I have a chance with acting. Ha. Maybe cos I say convincingly that I'm still hungry after a Big Mac, large fries, two apples pies, a sundae and a large chocolate milkshake.

She's smiling but I can see she wants to cry.

It's weird. It's usually me that does the crying.

We make a deal. That if I get into this new school, which she got me the prospectus for —

She told me that I was good enough for —

We made a deal, that if I got into this school and there were no incidents at home for three months we wouldn't have to do anymore meetings.

I mean, she was great.

She was a public servant.

She had loads of kids like me to deal with.

Similar stories, loads of paperwork to fill in.

This was her JOB.

In the eyes of the state, I was her customer, just a service user.

Another bruised smelly kid.

But.

She listened.

And I loved her.

My mates would interrupt my secnd apple pie by shouting 'Who's that ginger you're with?', in Mitcham Maccy D's.

And I'd nervously say, 'Oh my aunty', as she'd be writing her notes.

I didn't want these complications in my new school.

Maybe they would never have to know.

No one would.

I could start afresh.

There were dark times when I wanted to. . . .

but she changed that.

And she was so tall – or maybe I was just really small.

And I'll never see her again.

And I guess that's ok.

## 15. Alan

When I was fifteen, I had a hero, a friend. A role model. Alan. Every time I went to see my nan and grandad, I'd come and check for you. Everything about you was cool. Your tattoos, your rings, and your shaved head.

I remember going to your house and meeting your nan and grandad. Dunno if you remember, but I did meet your mum one time before she died.

(*As Alan's mum*) 'Alan! You're a cunt and I wish you were dead.'

I still remember the smell of your house. Your grandad used to paint everything white. There was always a strong smell of paint. You'd look down and he'd have painted his shoes white, clothes white, and the TV white. There was a picture of Princess Di torn out of the *TV Times*, stuck onto the bog wall, painted white! I promise you. I'll never forget the smell of that house. Yes, he was a bit nuts. But I know he loved you to bits. Your nan and grandad did everything they could to look after you.

I remember we used to walk around Balham and Clapham old town. You in your black bomber jacket which had orange lining, which was cool at the time. You used to talk about designer labels, and cars, and to be honest I didn't know anything about designer labels and cars, and I can't stand cars, but I used to listen thinking, 'Yeah, well he's really cool, so he knows about this stuff.' Seriously.

Man, you made me feel part of something. Protected. Like you weren't the biggest guy, but if anyone tried anything on, you would always tell them, 'You wot? FUCK OFF!'

Ah man, you used to crack me up.

When you kept getting tattoos, on your arms, hands, and even neck, I remember the day that I said to myself 'I'm gonna get tattoos on my hands and neck. Just. Like. Alan.'

Do you remember we used to always swap things? Everything, and anything. Watches, rings, fake chains, Nintendo cartridges. I swapped my

Sega Mega Drive for that York weights bench. I've been training ever since. I miss my Mega Drive though. You probably shot it by now.

My nan was actually very good friends with your nan.

'I've known Alan's grandparents his whole life. I've known him ever since he was a little baby. You need to stay away from him!'

You lived right by them, just off of Cavendish Road, and I didn't understand her beef.

We just carried on rolling, and I remember all that gear you used to have. I soon realised how you were getting it.

We were walking past a car near your baby mother's house, and I noticed that you picked up the most tiniest of stones and threw it at a car window. The glass shattered, but it was noiseless and the glass was in one piece. You pushed your hand through the window, opened the car door, and within thirty seconds had taken the stereo, an old jumper off the back seat, and some money out of the glove compartment. I was stunned, but excited at the same time. I felt part of something. Soon I realised that you were also robbing people's houses and back gardens. Even your bloody neighbour. Doing it didn't feel wrong though. I didn't consider myself a bad person when we were doing all of that, I was the lookout. I didn't think that I had done anything bad as I wasn't the one doing the smashing, I was just taking the stuff. What else did we have to do?

I think that the worst thing that we did, was that we jumped into gardens and nicked underwear because it was by Giorgio Armani. Pretty fucked up that we would nick underwear.

It felt like we had been boys for years, but it may have only been two summers before we lost contact. You just seemed to disappear. Then I got news.

'Conny, Alan has been caught with one hundred and nine E tablets and ten stolen car stereos whilst driving a nicked Ford Escort without a licence. He's going down, and down for a while. I *told* you to stay away from him!'

Alan. Man.

I meet Alan like, ten years later. He kinda looks the same. More tattoos, less hair. It's kinda weird because he was a couple of years older than me. For some reason, he thinks I'm still a teenager, like maybe nineteen, still on the cusp of doing great things. I said 'Alan, it was like ten years ago . . .'

He just shakes his head. Unbelievably.

Alan's grandparents had dementia, and mine were compos mentis.

Alan got caught, and I didn't. I was lucky really.

## 16. Miss Nelson

I changed school. Lucky for me because I had gone to a boys' school where the PE teacher Mr Hibbs actually called me a poof because I didn't like football or rugby. On top of that, he also called me queer, and so did the other boys because I didn't wanna take part in naked wrestling in the showers and whipping each other with towels. My parents wrote me a note exempting me from showers, backed up by Julie, who the school was a bit scared of.

Anyway, Julie helped get me into a selective school, where I was immediately out of my depth. The kids spoke differently, and everything I said would make people laugh. Just my normal talking. I don't know if it was all the swearing or what, but I was starting to hold court amongst many class mates, everyone watching and listening for the next crazy shit I was going to say and do.

There were also those who were looking down their nose at me from the very beginning. The school was non uniform, and my second hand and if I was lucky Asda George clothes stuck out amongst all the Versace, Moschino and D&G.

They would ask me what brand my trainers were when they actually knew, and when I would say 'Nicks', they would burst out laughing.

Anyway, this just made me act worse, and I was progressively getting more out of control swearing at teachers. I even took in a gun. I got suspended.

Well one teacher, Miss Nelson, she was telling me off after school. But she said, 'Everyone is talking about you, all the teachers. They are saying that you had so much promise, but you are throwing it away. You're better than that. Everyone is shocked at how much you have let yourself down, you know we care about you.'

Mum never bought us any books for school. I think she forgot or didn't realise or something.

I was trying to fight back the tears and keep my hard man stance as Miss Nelson pulled out a copy of *Hamlet* and said, 'This is for you. Keep it.'

I hated Shakespeare, but it was kind of cool to have something brand new. And mine. The one book I owned. Confusing, long and dark. The Prince of Denmark. Who thought the world was a prison, as long as he saw it that way.

She told me to take my drama and acting serious, and to read it. The whole thing.

The whole thing?!

This was shocking to me. My teacher seemed to really give a shit. She didn't have to.

She said I was special. That I had potential.

Still, I didn't get any GCSEs, but it did, for a time, calm me down. Even if she was lying.


**17.  Cotchin'** (*rapped*)

Cotchin'
I remember cotchin'
People living their lives
I was sitting watching
Barely taking it in
My adviser taking the piss
You should go look for a job
But all the jobs are shit
Cotchin'
I remember cotchin'
People living their lives
I was sitting watching
Barely taking it in
My adviser taking the piss
You should go look for a job
But all the jobs are shit
I was too late for education times three
But for me the spiel was the New Deal
Had to do courses about choices
My careers options
Often they didn't want to listen
I didn't want to be a cunt
But the position they wanted me to be in
Was barely living

I knew the precedent for my fate
Wasn't great
When I turned and saw all the little pricks
Up on my estate
Twenty-five-year-olds kicking beer cars to the wall
Only the drug dealers had the cash to look cool
Had thirty pound for the week
Went to the shop to get some sweets
Shop keep
Keeps watching
Gonna go back to cotchin'
Cotchin'
I remember cotchin'
People living their lives
I was sitting watching
Barely taking it in
My adviser taking the piss
You should go look for a job
But all the jobs are shit
Cotchin'
I remember cotchin'
People living their lives
I was sitting watching
Barely taking it in
My adviser taking the piss
You should go look for a job
But all the jobs are shit
Let's take it back
Summer time was the prime time
To get jacked
So you'd put on your fitted cap
The eyes are the window to the soul
So you would flip your cap low
I could hide away from danger it might sound pretty strange but
It was my invisible cloak
The code of the street so you wouldn't get beat
Yet people looking at me and imagine
I was doing some kind of impropriety
Without it
I would of got robbed
No doubt about it
They call us chavs

Council Housed And Violent
I just hated being denigrated and silenced
Cotchin'
I remember cotchin'
People living their lives
I was sitting watching
Barely taking it in
My adviser taking the piss
You should go look for a job
But all the jobs are shit
Cotchin'
I remember cotchin'
People living their lives
I was sitting watching
Barely taking it in
My adviser taking the piss
You should go look for a job
But all the jobs are shit

## 18. Advice to the Playa

When I left school with no GCSEs, some of the teachers were acting like I was gonna be a bum.

Strangely I never felt like a loser.

My mum cried.

I was the smartest person in the room, in my family. And I got nothing.

No passes. Not even in *drama*.

But I didn't feel like a failure. Even though I had reason to.

I was sixteen, so it was time for me to get a job or move out.

That was kinda the rules in my family.

My mum got me a job interview at the bus garage.

'Can you count?'

'No.'

'Are you trustworthy?'

'No . . . Not really.'

'Well. Your mum says that you are dying to get into the work of transport?'

And with that I was a fully-fledged bus conductor on a Routemaster bus.

I was always on time and often worked seven days a week, sometimes doing double shift which meant working for twenty hours straight.

I loved it. I was the youngest conductor on the fleet.

I was so excited that I went back to my old school to visit my mates in sixth form.

'Haha . . . That's a shit job . . . What a waste of a life . . . you're gonna be just like your mum.'

I never went back again. For a while I never really had any friends. They were at school or busy.

So I had quite a bit of disposable money.

I spent some of it on crap, often eating McDonald's every day – which was on my tick list of things I wanted to do when I was grown up and rich. And a LOT of CDs, cassettes and clothes. As well as Versace Blue Jeans, Hooch and N64 games.

But what I spent the majority of my money on was audio and recording equipment. I started off with a Fostex 4 track and Tascam 8 track, and then moved onto buying a PC and CD recording drive from a computer fair. I had never met anyone who could burn their own cd before, I could do it way before anyone. It crashed a lot and messed up a lot of disks, but it was sick. My own music on a disc.

I taught myself to make beats and how to sample. There was no YouTube back then, so I had to create my own system of sampling and looping. I promised that I would never tell people how I was doing it, and I never did. Quite a few record labels were interested in how and what I was doing, including Polydor Records and others.

I decided that I needed to meet and collaborate with other people, as I had spent two years on the buses, and I started South Thames College.

I never had the entrance grades, but the tutor said that my knowledge of music and drama was enough to get me in at the second level.

I was the only white boy in the class, which is saying something considering my dad is Indian.

I was scared shitless at first. STC was a bit different from my selective performing arts school. But I just remind myself that Tupac went to performing arts school and he was as hard as maths. And he was shot five times.

I immediately clashed with this kid playing a drama game. You had to sit down on chairs really fast and he bashed me out of the way. We both just stopped, glaring into each other's eyes. We were both either shit scared, or wanted to kill each other.

I was shit scared.

After this I never wanted to go back in.

But I did, and one day this kid was like, 'What you listening to?'

'Beats. My beats.'

And he just grabbed the headphones. 'Brap brap brap . . . boooooo. Heavy. Fucking dope.

'How did you make this? *You* made this?'

'Yeah.'

MC Gambit, aka Mister Mav.

Sounded like Method Man, with the flow of Redman. He could freestyle about anything for days. He was a genius.

We soon started hitting up my bedroom studio making tracks.

I started to help Gam to formulate his songs into bars, and how to double track vocals. I felt at home giving guidance about music and performance. Giving little tips about delivery.

> *Speak the speech I pray you*
> *As I pronounced it to you,*
> *Trippingly off the tongue.*
> *But if you mouth it*
> *As many of our players do*
> *I would lief the town crier spoke my lines.*
> *Be not too tame either, but let your own discretion be your tutor.*
> *Suit the action to the word, and the word the action, with this special observance,*
> *That you overstep not the modesty of nature.*

## 19. Not tears . . . Just something in my eyes

She is telling me that with my current attitude, I'm never going to make it as a performer.

If I can't be respectful enough to make it on time, this is never going to be a career for me.

'And that's ok. If you don't want this Conrad, that's fine. But it's sad that you have come this far to let yourself down and have a bad attitude. It seemed like you were happy to be here. Maybe I was wrong. Maybe you want to have this rude attitude, but that's not going to work here. Sorry.'

'Shit.'

I don't want to be another waste man from my estate. End up like that person in my dreams. But I repeatedly cast myself as the trouble maker, disrupting the class and cussing out the teacher.

'Not tears . . . just something in my eye.'

I was up late last night creating a madness. The police were called. I came in forty minutes late.

'Would *you* hire you Conrad?'

'No.'

Can't be tears. Just hayfever.

'Shit. . . . She believed in me and I've let her down.' For the first time I'm actually embarrassed about my attitude and behaviour. I do deserve to be kicked out. No one should hear my beats or see me perform. I'm a prick.

She's being horrible to me man. I feel like shit, but she seems to care about me.

Even though I've never felt this low.

And although at this moment I hate this bitch, she fucking cares about me.

And even though I've been a complete dick, she seems to think that there is more for me.

She gives me one more chance, and I HAVE to be early tomorrow.

I don't want to feel this embarrassed again. I don't want to let her down.

I'm never going to jepordise myself again like this. Never gonna create problems with the police again. (There was one more time. It was semi serious . . . and it was on my record for thirteen years . . . But my DBS is clean now!)

And I continue to wipe away whatever it is in my eye, all the way home on the 77 bus back to Mitcham.


## 20. DenMarked

Hamlet the Prince of Denmark is torn by raging feelings about his father, and the treachery of his mother. Throughout the play he wrestles with his feelings about life, death and his significance in the wider universe. He struggles to know what he should think and feel about the events that are engulfing his spirit. Early on in the play he greets Rosencrantz and Guildenstern, two visitors to the royal Danish court.

He welcomes them with these words.

> *My excellent friends! How dost thou Guildenstern?*
> *Good lads, how do you both?*
> *What have you my good friends, deserved at the hands of fortune that*
> *she sends you to prison hither?*

Guildenstern is surprised. He asks Hamlet what he means by calling here prison.

Hamlet says '*Denmark's a prison.*'

Rosencrantz laughs and says that if that's true, then the whole world is a prison.

Hamlet says that it is.

Rosencrantz says '*We think not my lord.*'

Hamlet's reply is profound.

> *'Tis none for you, for there is nothing either good nor bad but*
> *thinking makes it so. To me it is a prison.*

So Sophie. Blonde woman, around thirty, casually dressed, finally came at around 10.37, and we went into the theatre of the school. She was apologising for it, but it was better than most theatre spaces I had ever seen.

'Your CV is remarkable', she said. 'We have interviewed five people for this role, but you are perfect.'

Then after she asked me some questions, she asked me if I wanted the job. Just like that. Just asked me. She didn't even mention the coffee cup. And I almost left an uncomfortable silence thinking about all the reasons why it was totally implausible for me to get the job before saying, 'Yes. Yes, I think this is right for me.'

She told me I should fit right in and she'd see me on Monday. Then she asked if I had read *King Lear*.

FUCK!

Then she said, 'No, no . . . it's *Hamlet* they are doing.'

And I said, 'Yeah, Yeah I know that one.'

## 21.  The Dream Goes On (*sung/rapped*)

*And the dream goes on*
*In my mind today*
*I feel I will obey*

*I see my father*
*Standing in front of me*
*He is everything*
*They say that I will be*
*But I want to change*
*I am my own man*
*I'm trying to keep untying*
*My vision and my history*
*And be what I can be*

*And the dream goes on*
*In my mind today*
*I feel I will obey*

*I see my reflection*
*Shining in front of me*
*He has everything*
*That I will ever need*
*I don't need to change*
*I'm my own man*
*I'm changing my vision*
*The world is no longer my prison*
*If I see it that way*
*My dreams can change*

*And the dream goes on*
*In my mind today*
*I feel I will obey*

I still get the dream
But from now on
I'll change my vision up
I see it how I wanna see it
To be or not to be it
'Tis thinking makes it so
So I change up my dreams
No longer marked
By the past
I'm DenMarked.

*At end of song* **Conrad** *live beatboxes, walking to the centre of the stage.*

*End.*

# High Rise eState of Mind

David Bonnick Jr, Paul Cree, Lakeisha Lynch-Stevens
and Conrad Murray

First performed as a full-length play at Battersea Arts Centre on 20 March 2019.

Recordings of the raps, songs and musical numbers for this production are available on various streaming sites, including Spotify (*High Rise eState of Mind* by Beats & Elements), and SoundCloud (*High Rise eState of Mind* by Conrad Murray).

## Character List (original cast)

At points in the production the cast step out of character and play themselves in 'Real World Moments'. In these places the actors' names are indicated in the script.

| | | |
|---|---|---|
| **Tony** | *Facilities manager* | (Paul Cree) |
| **Luke** | *Twenties male, Anglo-Indian* | (Conrad Murray) |
| **David** | *Doctor, thirties / forties* | (David Bonnick Jr) |
| **Michelle** | *Twenties female* | (Lakeisha Lynch-Stevens) |

## Creative Team

| | |
|---|---|
| *Lighting Designer/ Stage Manager* | Simeon Miller |
| *Movement Director* | Akeim Toussaint Buck |
| *Producer* | Sarah Blowers (Strike A Light), with Battersea Arts Centre, Camden People's Theatre and GL4 as producing partners |

## Opening Announcement

**Tony** (*Spoken. Line breaks indicate a slight musicality/rhythm to the language.* **Tony** *speaks with a robotic intonation, at points where* **Tony** *narrates, his cap is turned forwards, where he interacts with other characters, his cap is turned backward*s):

This is a facilities services'
announcement. I'd like to welcome
all of our new residents moving
into our exclusive middle floor,
apartments, you have made an
excellent acquisition, welcome to
the future.
Our architects and designers are
delighted with what they've
created, bespoke apartments fit for
only those who've worked hard and
wish to enjoy life's finest
pleasures. Access to all facilities
on floors twenty-four and below are free for
you to enjoy, at all times.
For those of you with the ultimate
ambition, to one day reside in our
top floor apartments, please note
one occupant will be hand selected
to apply by our upper chamber of
unelected faceless delegates, upon completion
of ten years residency. However,
all top floor occupancies are
currently full, they say God
himself has so far been
unable to obtain an
apartment . . . that's a joke.
To our new lower floor residents
you are part of our Mark One
apartments. You are extremely
fortunate that you have been
relocated, to live in our wonderful
community. Please note, your entry
and exit into the building will be
via the exclusive, steel enforced

Mark One door situated at the rear of
the building. Access to any floor
above yours is prohibited, except
when visiting the doctors' surgery.
Your communal kitchen and washing
facilities meet the absolute
minimum requirements, as laid out
by the National Party of Social
Liberal guidelines. For those of
you receiving financial assistance,
you will access these via the
Ubiquitous Merit System Terminal,
located by the exit door. Whilst
you remain in the Mark One
apartments, please meditate upon the
following:
'Hard work, pays off.'

**Looking Up** (*musical number*)

**Luke** (*sung*)

We're looking up
They're looking down
We're looking up
They're looking down
We're looking we're looking
We're looking up
They're looking down
We're looking up
They're looking down
We're looking we're looking
We're looking up
They're looking down
We're looking up
They're looking down
We're looking we're looking
We're looking up
They're looking down
We're looking up
They're looking down
We're looking we're looking

**Tony** (*rapped*)

Welcome to City Heights
It's the pinnacle of civil engineering design
Modern metropolitan living now
redefined
An architectural tribute to mankind.
Utopia in the skies
We invite you to rise,
From the ground floor the lift glides
Take in the sights
No need to step outside
Everything you need, we provide
State of the art facilities are all
on site
Leisure, education even catering too,
Only the finest organic produce delivered to you
Part of our service to nourish our
Residents' bodies and minds
Let your children get their
Schooling while you unwind
Walk the walk-ways be inspired,
Spiritually climb,
Let the individual flourish we
encourage one to rise
The future's arrived and we defined
it City Heights
Don't delay book a viewing today
and change your life.

**All** (*sung*)

We're looking up
They're looking down
We're looking up
They're looking down
We're looking they're looking

**Luke** (*rapped*)

Sitting here in the spot
So many people hoping they can get to the
top
I just feel lucky
to have a home
and a mobile phone,

Someone to call my own.
Well, Michelle, she's ill,
Like literally and metaphorically
Netflix and chill,
With the boxsets.
The only thing is she gets
kinda stressed with the lack of
heating.
And a couple of doors down
the neighbours always beefing
Leaky ceiling, we ain't got a lot,
but we don't need more,
At least we got our own front door.

**All** (*sung*)

We're looking up
They're looking down
We're looking up
They're looking down
We're looking they're looking
We're looking up
They're looking down
We're looking up
They're looking down
We're looking they're looking

**David** (*rapped*)

Look around
Wow!
Can't believe I'm here and this is
happening now
My own place that I call mine
Top floor by design
One of a kind.
Look, look Mum I made it,
I raised the funds
Imagine that!
Your grown-up son.
Though you never had a doubt
what I would become
You gave me the strength to believe
it could be done.
So, let's have a drink and celebrate at the

balcony
Take in the view of the city, look where we
Raised from the ground like
The flower out the cracks
To top floor luxury flats
Imagine that!
Elected by the board
Top city practice
Name on the deed
Of this Zone One property,
I gave this to you because
you gave it all to me
And now I'm here,
On top of the city
As we're . . . .

**All** (*sung*)

We're looking up
They're looking down
We're looking up
They're looking down
We're looking they're looking

*End song.*

**Michelle** (*spoken with slight rhythm*)

Just squeezed in to these walls,
fob key works properly, we've been
Reassured –
'Facilities, warmth and comfort,
support led by the
National Party of Social Liberals.'
End quote.
We arrived. Me and Luke and some
dude with a pram by his side.
By our luggage was his buggy that I
guess he bought for Carla.
He's her first son's father. Lil
Arthur
Turns six on the seventeenth.
Carla invited me and Luke to the
gathering,
She lives on our floor too
by the section for showering,

With her three kids and she's proud
of it.
And I'm a bit – not jealous but I'm
a little stressed,
Cos me and Luke aren't better than
other residents
But even Luke's mum,
Who's never made even enough to
pay her tax stamp,
Told me – if he's slacking – just
don't have that.
And it's not that –
It's not like I don't love Luke
I do
He is lovely and he's different
But I love living
In the real world too
I do
You see we waited
ten months for this place
And it's shit
But the look on his face
As we emptied one small case
And ate a bag of chips
On the first night
Haunted me.
How could he be so happy?
Seriously.
Shit.
I'm not Daddy's little princess
Daddy couldn't care less
But it's like this is not what I
thought
Life would be like by twenty-three.
It's not that I ain't happy,
But sometimes
When I'm sitting there
dreaming about the future
And he's just staring at me
Smiling
I wonder what he is smiling for.
It's not like I don't love Luke,
I do . . .

## Real World Moment 1 – Estates

**Conrad** (*spoken*)    I tell Mum that I'm going to play out back, but she says, 'You can't go Croydon'. Yeah. As if. Croydon's too far to walk to from Mitcham anyway. I take the chain latch (which doesn't seem to do anything) off, and walk out onto the balcony. I imagine that when people leave their houses, people who live on roads, they feel free. Out in the wild.

Not so on Laburnham.

You're outside, but you are out on the balcony, looking at all the front doors that are exactly the same, just at different levels of disrepair. (A bit like us really.)

Still on the estate.

I walk into the lift, the metal door just about managing to open, and instantly feel the sting of piss. It just hits you. I'll never get over that instant sting to the eyes. And the way your trainers stick to the floor. Why would anyone do that in their own lift?

What does it even mean?

It's dark. The street lights are out. Head down, no eye contact. I'm not scared. I know everyone. Who the dealers are, who to not fuck with. I'm not scared.

I'm not *that* scared.

There's no police about, because they never seem to come near.

They don't know we exist. No one does.

Well, they do when someone off of the estate accuses one of us lot of stealing something. And when they want our votes.

There's rubbish all dumped in one corner right by a 'Fly-tippers Will Be Prosecuted' sign. I think they see that sign as a dare. It's a fucking disgrace. To be honest, there are no bins, and sometimes I throw my shit on there too.

'Oi Fatty – buss me a dollar.' Jason Rock's dad has just gone jail. I don't feel sorry for him as he is currently robbing me. Not of a dollar but of twenty pence aka two Chomp bars, or two Freddos to be exact. To be fair he does say, 'Safe, yeah'. (That means thank you.)

I must be a sorry sight, head down, no eye contact, crying.

Do estates let people down, or do people let the estates down?

I don't know . . .

I see a familiar face! Iain Wilson says we should go on a trip. He met some girl at the swimming pool. And She. Wants. To 'do it!'.

This is exciting.

Trouble is . . . there's a catch. It was in Croydon. CR7.

Yeah, there are hot girls in Croydon. But it's embargoed territory.

I can't even believe Iain is here, his mum says he's not allowed onto the estate.

I decide that even though the Whitgift Centre sounds exciting, and there's the temptation of vicariously experiencing some kind of sexual contact by watching my friend, which is not creepy but the thing teenage dreams are made of, I can't leave.

I never leave anyway.

Even when I do, it's like I haven't. I'm just in post-estate mode. It has you in a way. You're part of it. Part of the buildings and the walk-ways. I tell him, 'Next time'. He says something like, 'She had a friend for you as well' and walks off.

I walk back past the kids playing night football by the 'No Ball Games' sign, hands in my pockets, nodding to the people it's needed for me to acknowledge.

Head down: no direct eye contact.

I look up to my block. One day I'm gonna leave this place. No more sticky lifts. No more getting jacked, no more mates that shouldn't be here.

I tell my mum to let me in, and promise her that I never even thought about going to Croydon.

**David and Tony Part 1** (*rapped over instrumental*)

**Tony**

> Mr David
> On behalf of City Heights
> Welcome to the middle floor,
> Twenty-four flights
> Mr David
> Please,

Take in all the sights.
These are your first steps
To a better life.

**David**

Erm, thank you, and your name is?

**Tony**

Mr David
Apologies
I've no manners,
Tony is my name
Facilities manager.
Mr David
Are you all settled in?
I'm here for you
Should you need anything?

**David**

Tony, thank you, yes I'm David.
I just moved in
And it's so spacious.
Tony, I'm moved, the views, amazing
I've just called my mum,
I can't believe I made it.

**Tony**

Mr David,
I'm happy you approve.
The architect designed it
To fit around you.

**David**

Tony, it's a dream come true,
Everything seems wonderful and new.

**Tony**

Mr David,
I believe there were
themes
Gothic, Venetian
and the seven seas

**David**

> Tony, I don't know art history,
> But it looks wonderful
> if you ask me.

**Tony**

> Mr David, nor am I an art critic
> Though I do like doing
> Dot to dot pictures.

**David**

> Tony, dot to dot pictures?!
> I'm in stiches
> You're not serious?

**Tony**

> Mr David.
> I'm very serious.

*Cut music.*

**David**

> Tony, excuse my ignorance.

*Bring music back in.*

**Tony**

> Mr David, should you need me
> Anytime of the day
> Please ring me.

**David**

> Tony, I'm fine, I'm easy
> But it's handy
> to know your
> availability.

**Tony**

> Mr David
> It's my duty to serve
> City Heights maintenance is
> My life's work,

From the ground floor
to the top floor
it's my church,
Service of the tower is the faith I
observe.

**David**

Tony, I just don't have the words,
It's so perfect, it's absurd!
And this is the middle floor?
From what I've heard
The top floor is just like heaven
on earth?

**Tony**

Mr David, I couldn't possibly
comment,
If you suffer from heights then I
wouldn't recommend.

*Cut beat out.*

**David**

Tony, was that one a joke?

**Tony**

Yes, It was a joke.

*Pause.*

*Bring beat back in.*

**David**

Tony, you're funny my friend,
Thank you, and thank you, and thank you
again.
By the way, David is just fine,
Mr David just doesn't feel right.

**Tony**

David, sorry, I'll ensure I get it
right,
Using people's titles is a habit
of mine.

**David**

> Tony, in that case, call me Dr,
> Just qualified, a physician for my
> crimes.

**Tony**

> Doctor,
> I'm in need of some advice.

**David**

> Tony, you can ask me any time.

*Cut beat out.*

**Tony**

> I have a bad case of pubic lice.

**David**

> Joke?

**Tony**

> No joke.

**David**

> Tony, I'm sure a simple cream
> will suffice.

*Bring beat back in.*

**Tony**

> Doctor, well then I'll be on my way
> Remember you can contact me
> night or day.

**David**

> Tony, was a pleasure all the same
> I'm happy to know that hard work
> really pays.

**Cheeky Chopsticks** (*musical number*)

**Michelle** (*sung*)

> Wannabe up, wannabe out

Wanna be anywhere but here Luke.
Do you hear Luke?

**Luke** (*sung.*)

Yeah.
All right.

**Michelle** (*sung*)

Cos this place is too packed as it is.
Do they have to share a toilet?
Cos somebody's pissing in the lift!
And next door's got seven kids,
and I hear their mother screaming
every time, they're getting hit.
We don't do that over here.

**Luke** (*sung*)

Hold on.
Slow down.
They wanna get out, wanna get up,
wanna be getting on right here babes.
They're the same as us, babes.

**Michelle** (*sung*)

No.

**Luke** (*sung*)

Yeah.

**Michelle** (*sung*)

But it ain't the same tho,
Ain't spending the same dough,
Know they're on the social,
Kids grow anti-social,
Used to feel so hopeful,
Now I feel so hopeless.
Time we addresss our
Current address.

**Luke** (*sung*)

Come over here.

**Michelle** (*spoken*)   Alright babes.

**Luke** (*sung*)

    Forget about it.

**Michelle** (*spoken*)    Ah you think you are cute.

**Luke** (*sung*)

    Forget about it.

**Michelle** (*rapped*)

    We'll talk about it later Luke.

**Luke** (*sung*)

    Ok.

**Michelle** (*rapped*)

    Moving up soon, much bigger rooms.

**Luke** (*sung*)

    Ok

**Michelle** (*rapped*)

    I'm sick of the same shit here

**Luke** (*sung*)

    Ok

**Michelle** (*rapped*)

    Yo Luke you got cloth in your ears?

**Luke** (*sung*)

    I got some money, let me take you out,
    We'll go to cheeky Chopstix,
    Girl it's my shout.

**Michelle** (*sung/spoken*)

    Luke what you on?
    What you on?
    I don't trust Chinese food made by white people and Indians.

**Luke** (*sung*)

    What?
    Girl I'm Anglo-Indian!

**Michelle** (*sung*)

    Do you cook for me?

**Luke** (*spoken*)    No.

**Michelle** (*sung*)

Do you cook for me?

**Luke** (*spoken*)    No.

**Michelle** (*sung*)

Can we go out? Go out?
Can we, can we go out?

**Luke** (*spoken*)    Alright babes . . .

*End song.*


## Real World Moment 2

**Paul**    I'm from a big family. I grew up in a house with nine people in it, I had to share pretty much everything. Personal space was something I didn't have much of and my own space was something I always wanted. I didn't want a mansion or anything like that, just a little space that I could call mine.

Not long after I first left home, I got my own space – a little one room bedsit. I'd made it. It was mouldy, cold and smelled of wet towels – I hate that smell – and I could barely afford it.

I learned right there and then that space, or decent space, especially in the South East, very much comes at a premium. So in order to move out, I got a second job and moved into a nicer flat with a mate from school. Sharing again.


## How Long?

**Luke** (*sung*)

How long is it gonna be?
How long is it gonna be?
How long is it gonna be?
How long is it gonna be?

**Tony** (*rapped*)

They see the lift
but they don't
see the shaft
They think there's no ceiling
but they don't see the glass

There's metal rungs and there's
sharp shards
but they only see the sparkle
or their face
if they look hard
They see the movement but they
don't see the mechanisms,
Intricate parts well-greased, cogs,
wheels and pistons.
They see the personnel,
but don't attend the meetings
They smell the coffee but they
don't taste the caffeine,
They see the people below and note
the difference
They amplify the distance to make
it significant
They build barriers, begin to
build resistance
Lines get drawn between floors of
existence
They speak about aspiration and
aiming high
Yet they're all looking down their necks
or leaning to the side
They say they wanna rise and make
it to the top but
They've never seen the floor where
the lift finally stops

**All** (*sung*)

How long is it gonna be?
How long is it gonna be?

**Michelle** (*rapped*)

So,
Tim.
Tim put me through to Helen,
Who copied in the lady,
Who told me wait on Sharon.
Sharon saw my email and told me to
write a letter,
Said I needed credit checks and
references – I let her, do her

thing.
Ring –
Back through to Tim.
'Sorry love, Mark One enquiry's not
my thing'
So, then what?
How long's it gonna take?
'If you've already sent your letter
off – you'll just –
you'll have to wait'
Hung up – what a fucking bellyache,
It's too early for a mug when
I've barely even ate.
And since I got this new zero-hour
contract,
I'm still waiting for the prick to
make contact.
All them interviews and
training days they hosted,
DBS got processed – passed and now
they've ghosted.
Fed up, of all these admin hiring
fakes,
Before that – it's all grins and
handshakes.
I mean – in bold, on the top you
can see,
'Business Psychology'
right across my CV.

*Sung*

How long is it gonna be?

**Luke** (*rapped*)

Generation rent
All the time spent learning
Young minds inspired heart's burning
Now was it worth it?
Working for what?
What's the purpose?
We gave a hundred per cent,
Why you wanna hurt us?
We're the real earners
Generation rent!

**All** (*shouted*)

WE'RE THE REAL EARNERS!

**Luke** (*call*)

Generation rent

**All** (*response*)

WE'RE THE REAL EARNERS!

**Luke** (*rapped*)

We gave a hundred per cent, why you wanna hurt us?

**David** (*sung*)

I've been waiting,
I've been waiting for a long time
I've been waiting,
it's taking most of my life.
I've been waiting and the time's
ticking and I've been patient and I
can't take it going through the
paces through the rat races yeah
I've been waiting
I hate it
I've been waiting,
I've been waiting for a long time.

*End song.*

**David and Tony Part 2: Lightbulbs** (*rapped over instrumental*)

**David**

Tony, my friend, how are you?

**Tony**

Doctor
Marvellous – and you?

**David**

Tony, I feel at home already
I am in luxury yet still quite edgy
Tony, I love the rooms,
love the views,
But there's just one thing
I need to ask you.

**Tony**

Doctor, you can ask me anything you
like

**David**

Tony, the lightbulbs, they're too
bright
Just a fraction of too much
light
Tony, I like them but they're
not right,
Could you possibly
change them when you've got time?

**Tony**

Doctor, I will change them right away.

**David**

Tony, I'm happy to wait.

**Tony**

Doctor,
I've just re-scheduled my whole
day
In 2.92 hours they'll be changed.

**David**

Tony, that's, erm . . . GREAT!

**Tony**

Doctor you're welcome
I'll be on my way.

**David**

Tony, you are really are a saint,
by the way . . .

*Beat cuts out.*

**David** (*cont'd*)

How is your erm issue?

**Tony**

Issue?

**David**

The itchy, crabs, crotch, issue?

**Tony**

Doctor, cream worked a dream, thanks to
you.

**David**

Excellent Tony.
Wonderful.

**Tough at the Top** (*musical number*)

**Luke** (*sung*)

It's tough
At the top
Do you wanna go?
(Do you wanna go)
It moves so fast
It won't stop
We can't make it slow.
Do you wanna go?
Today was just yesterday's dream
It still doesn't seem
Quite the picturesque scene
What will remain
if we get what we want, but me and
you change?
We never used to need much,
We never had things, close my eyes and
it stings,
Yesterday's gone, how do we know if
we've got it all wrong?
It's tough,
At the top,
Do you wanna go?
It moves so fast
It won't stop
We can't make it slow
Do you wanna go?
Can anybody see down here?
Sipping in their rarefied air

Wondering if they still care
What will remain?
If we get what we want
But me and you change?
We never used to need much
We never had things
I close my eyes and it stings.
But yesterday's gone,
How do we do we know if we've done
it all wrong?
It's tough,
At the top,
Do you wanna go?
It moves so fast,
It won't stop . . . .
We can't make it slow
Do you wanna go?

*End song.*

## Real World Moment 3

**Jr**    So, my real name is David Bonnick Jr, aka, Gambit Ace. I live at home with my mum at the moment. I can't afford to move out to my own place. Our home is a building with three flats, and we live on the middle floor. The children I grew up with are both in relationships, and both have children of their own, and they would constantly laugh at me for not moving out. The funny thing is, that after a year, both couples had to move back to their parents' home because they couldn't afford the rent that they were paying. But do you know what's funny? . . . Do you know what's really funny? . . .

They're not laughing at me anymore.

## What Floor? (*musical number*)

**Luke** (*sung*)

What floor are we on?
How do we get off?
And does God know that we're here?

(*Rapped*)

Tired of the rain,
Tired of the pain,
Tired of having to explain

that even though we complain
Still there's no change.
Tired of the wars
Tired of the postcodes,
Tired of the same coloured doors,
I'm tired of all the floors.
The rubbish stuck in the chute,
Is like a metaphor for the youth,
Summer's over,
Few people make it onto the roof,
Living in close quarters,
whether we like it or not
The zeitgeist of the heights,
seen through the whites of the eyes of the kids,
What's the cost of architectural holocaust?
Habitat of the lost cause,
Maybe we deserve
To traverse these perverse paths,
It's a joke
But somehow we're all missing the laughs.

**Luke** (*sung*)

What floor are we on?
How do we get off?
And does God know that we're here?

**Tony** (*rapped*)

Ask yourself the question
How did we get here?
I dare you, double dare you
The truth is out there
A designer vest top from a posh
boutique in Mayfair probably
descends from a sweatshop where
asbestos plagues the air.
That planning application for that
extension on your abode
Did you encroach on your neighbour's
territory in advancement of your
own?
How did we get here how did you get
there and did you play fair or were

there rules? Or was it canine
eating canine and what was left
went on to go and rule?
Did you tell yourself you deserved it?
Did you tell yourself yourself you were worth it?
Did you tell yourself you're a self
made success and help is worthless?
Only worthy of the shirkers
twitching curtains all nervous cos
the neighbours are straight out the
circus: thieves thugs, rapists and
murderers.
Everything you got you earned it,
worked for it, worked harder,
worked harder than hard stressed
heart triple bypass and now time's
passed and you might ask how did we
get here, with the nice car and all
the best gear?
What lurks in the shadow of the
rear view what you left behind for
that big career
How did we get here?

**Luke** (*sung*)

What floor are we on?
How do we get off?
And does God know that we're here?

*End Song.*

**Who is She?** (*musical number, rapped*)

**David**

Who is she?
Come on
Who is she?

**Tony**

You saw her in the lift
The other day it wasn't busy
I've seen her in the building
Just roaming around

**David**

> With that face so beautiful
> No sign of a smile
> Thought to myself
> I can make her be happy
> Said to myself
> I can see us being together
> Early morning breakfast
> Caviar with toast.
> Evenings
> Wining and dining
> Dark blue skies behind us
> I will take her to another height
> Another level
> Make her feel first class
> In the first class
> As we travel
>
> Do you know if she's single?

**Tony**

> I don't know that.

**David**

> Daffodils or red roses?

**Tony**

> I have no facts.

**David**

> I know she will accept
> An invitation to a dinner-date.
> Have the chef prepare
> A three course meal at eight.

**Tony**

> At yours?

**David**

> Yes mine.
> You should arrange the time.
> But most importantly,

That woman has to be mine!
She will be mine,
She's stuck in my mind
She has to be mine
I already know it
She is constantly on my mind
Like, all of the time
And I shall let her know it.
For real.

## Michelle

Like dark blue skies,
Like sun at night,
My heart took flight,
He's tall, brown eyes
'He called?'
Like twice
He's nice, he's wise
His balls have size
That can – re-populise all the
Stale dead memories I wanna lay to
rest
Gucci handbags, nothing but the best
Like song samples of what comes
next
Doctor's wages covering my nest.
Doctor's payslips covering my neck,
Doctor's crazy covering my cheques,
Luke can't pay this
covering your cheques
And when he says something he does
it with his chest.
We did it.
'Caviar and toast'
We did it!
And it was so so vivid.
And he did the most when he hit it.
And it was so so genuine, how he
asked me,
all these questions – gave
attention,
To all my innermost tensions.

'What did he ask then?'
Nothing in the past tense.
'Are you inspired by Luke?'
'How you gonna last then?'
'You're a grown woman – you're twenty-three.
Went to uni, bursaries for poverty
You got loans, before you got a
property.
Spend your life borrowing? Do it
properly.
And I have to ask.
Just to make it last,
Washing up liquid filled with
water . . .
Does he know that you're someone's
daughter?'
He said, 'Do you wanna look back,
Look back and know that you chose this?
You're like progress,
Sleeping with the enemy
But you're grown
You're smart
You're twenty-three.'

*End song.*

**Loser Like Your Mum** (*musical number, sung*)

**Luke**

Applied for the course
Finished the course
But of course, it doesn't mean shit
babes.
Cos I'm a piece of shit babe . . .

**Michelle**

Yeah.

**Luke**

I'm writing to my MP,
I voted for you,
So it's time that you did something for me
Cos its all my fault apparently,
When he's on the news

And he's claiming for fifty-five p.
They don't do shit round here.

**Michelle**

Hold on
Slow down
You sit on your arse
Don't get out of bed
Blame it all on everyone else
Babe
But it's all your fault babe.

**Luke**

No

**Michelle** (*spoken*)    All right.

**Luke**

But it ain't the same tho
we used to be the same tho
now you're being spiteful
used to be so mindful.

**Michelle**

I was nothing like you
Never took the time to
Never had a vision
Bastard drunk ambition
Love without condition.

**Luke**

Stop it Michelle listen

**Michelle**

You're a loser like your mum

**Luke**

Michelle talk to me

**Michelle** (*spoken*)    No.

**Luke**

Michelle talk to me

**Michelle** (*spoken*)    No.

**Luke**

>Can we work it out – out, can we –
>can we – can we work it out?

*End song.*


**Real World Moment 4**

**Lakeisha**    My mum's sixty-eight and still works two jobs to pay rent for the house she's lived in for over thirty years. She asked if I could buy it. Says it's too late for her. If I could afford to mortgage the house, I'd either never move out or have to organise a stranger to live there with her, to help me.

I tell her I worry about how much she works at her age. She says it's better than people that lay around doing nothing. I tell her there's no power in looking down on those that don't work because you work hard. You need to work smart. Some people make more than what she makes in five seven-to-twelve-hour days over the course of two days.

Are you working hard or working smart?

**So Sick** (*musical number, rap*)

**All**

>So sick
>Keep on going
>And you ain't ever gonna quit
>never never never
>You so sad
>Preeing on your being
>And you must be mad.

**Luke**

>I wanna be proper
>A gentleman
>Old school
>Happy Shopper
>When I go left
>I wonder is it so right
>Why does it feel so dark
>When I walk out into the light?
>Buildings don't let people down,

People let the buildings down
We draw the lines on a map
How fucked up is that?
We're not them
We are other
They call us names
We kill our brothers
Don't go out
Stay in
Never leave my room
Throw my hopes in the bin!

**All**

So sick
Keep on going
And you ain't ever gonna quit
NEVER NEVER NEVER
You so sad
Preeing on your being
And you must be mad.

**Michelle**

Luke you're not well,
You're not yourself
There's a doctor on the middle
floor said he could help
Sitting indoors curtains drawn
looking at porn instead of looking
for jobs to help yourself
It's not right,
you're not right in the head
When was the last time we made love
in our bed?
Making me feel like I've dried up
between my legs
But it's not me that can't get it
erect
It's not right you're not right in
the mind
It's been weeks since you've gone
outside
You talk about clothes but there's

no design
There's no way you're gonna blow
I'll blow your mind
By the way you'll go blind if you
keep it up
Compared to me your right hand gets
more love
We make love
but you can't keep it up
You're sick your need help
Luke do it for us.

**All**

Boy you so sick
Keep on going
And you ain't ever gonna quit
NEVER NEVER NEVER
You so sad
Preeing on your being
And you must be mad.

**David**

I can tell that you're not well
looking at your body
you're not right in your
self
You seem so negative about
everything that's a sure fire sign
that you need medicine
Late night playing games on the net
looking at porn yet during sex
can't stay erect you're addicted
that's a sure sign you're
depressed
Sign this form, take these meds
Wanna regain your prowess in the bed?
Take these meds
Wanna again feel fresh in your head?
Take these meds
Wanna again get out of your bed?
Take these meds
Wanna regain your girlfriend's

respect?
Take these meds
Follow the plan take these for nine months
At the end you'll see me again and
we'll review
Until then
just keep taking them
And one day,
You'll feel better again
You'll feel better again
You'll feel better again
You'll feel better again.

**All**

Boy you so sick
Keep on going
And you ain't ever gonna quit
NEVER NEVER NEVER
You so sad
Preeing on your being
And you must be mad.

*End song.*


**Real World Moment 5**

**Paul**    Since I first left home, I recently worked out that I've moved
eighteen times, with multiple different addresses. In one nutty year I
moved four times. I've lived on my own, but I've mainly had to share.
It's all right, I made my peace with sharing, it's a necessity after all.

It was whilst I was out with my girlfriend one afternoon that I realised
how much all this moving about has affected me. I was stood outside this
shop, in East Dulwich, Lordship Lane, near to where I was living at the
time, whilst she was inside browsing.

It was the sort of shop you often find in more affluent places in the trendy
parts of town, the sort of shop that sells a tea towel with a swear word on
it and charges twenty-five pounds.

I was wondering why it was that I always preferred to stand outside
while she was inside, browsing. It's not the fact that I'm not really
interested in what they sell, or that they tend to be quite expensive – it's
the fact that most of the stuff inside is designed for decorating a home. I

don't feel like I've had a home, since I first left home seventeen addresses ago. I've tried but it's quite difficult to make a place feel like home, when I always know that in the back of my mind, it belongs to someone else and that I'm probably gonna leave again.

**I Got it All** (*musical number, rapped*)

**All**

>We got it all
>stacking it up and we want
>more and more
>We got it all in
>We're all working hard
>So I guess we can all win.

**Luke**

>Even on a morning when I feel great
>Have to tell myself
>Not enough on my plate
>You can do better
>Make more cheddar
>More cake
>Got no ingredients
>Don't know how to bake
>Dreaming 'bout Courvoisier
>From Corbusier vantage
>Showing off
>Must give me advantage
>Hard work pays off
>I've given it all
>I must be a boss.

**Michelle**

>To-ny popped round yes-ter-
>day, I
>Didn't know how to say, what
>I'm doing in a-noth-er space.
>My mo-ther's face, my cousin's
>praise,
>The count-less days, I spent
>De-fla-ted,
>Now I made it.

Planted seeds – forest trees
Things I need – in front of me
Every single thing I eat's fucking
healthy
I'm brainy, and doc's wealthy.
Didn't spend three years on my
bachelors,
To be a female nag with a spatula,
Male nags, do the same,
We call them leeches, call them
Draculas.
Salary, new role – I got that.
Security and pension – got that.
Middle floor gym pass – got that.
And a mattress fit for my back.
Sharon called bout that job – fuck
that,
Looking at my phone like who's
that?
Memory foam, no springs in my back,
Doctor's seeing me as his match.

**All**

We got it all
stacking it up and we want
more and more
We got it all in
We're all working hard
So we can all win.

**David**

For each day of the year I got a
pair of socks
For each day of the week I've got a
different watch
For each minute of squash I got a
different top
For each second I reckon I've got a
food box
Never need to leave my flat again
I got food to feed a thousand men
Then feed I 'em again and again and

again
Feed the world like the world's my
friend
I got it all
Look Mum I got it all
Everything you'd ever need inside
of these walls
Can't believe I was ever even one
of them fools
Living in squalor because they
can't even pick up a tool
I worked hard, and hard work pays
off
Everything I got I deserve because
I put in work
On the bottom they got nothing
that's what they deserve
Everything you see, I earned!

**All**

We got it all
stacking it up and we want
more and more
We got it all in
We're all working hard
So we can all win.

*End song.*

**Tough at the at Top Part 2** (*musical number*)

**David** (*rapped*)

I deserve it, can't they see me
I want to smash through, every
ceiling
Till they hear me, and revere me
Undeniable aristocratic pedigree
Top of the tallest tree, notoriety
Intelligentsia secret societies
They'll document my rise throughout
history
The greatest minds all created a
dynasty
Except they won't let me in, I NEED IN

I've got it all except this one
thing
I'm so close to the greatest of
wins I've got
My finger in the air praying for a
change of wind
But the winds don't change they
remain
Day-to-day still looking out the
window pane
I'll scale the wall and I'll sever
and maim and
I'll use their blood to paint
murals of my name.

**Luke** (*sung*)

It's tough, at the top, do you
wanna go?
It moves so fast, it won't stop
we can't make it slow
do you wanna go?

**Tony** (*rapped*)

Doctor, you deserve it
So earnest, so virtuous
You've worked for it, so you will
earn it
You will rise like spirits in the
churches
In your service I've experienced
your worthiness
The top floor will adore your
assertiveness
Walls adorned in fine art so
luxurious
So much class you'll be running
at a surplus
But you first must believe in
yourself
Look in the mirror and see for
yourself
Is this a man who attracts life's

Wealth?
Is this a man the embodiment of
Health?
The answer's yes, Doctor!
Let me hear you say, Yes Doctor!

**David** (*shouted*)

YES!

**Tony** (*spoken*)    Louder Doctor.

**David** (*shouted*)

YES, YES, YES, I AM THE GREATEST!

**Luke** (*sung*)

It's tough, at the top, do you
wanna go?
It moves so fast it won't stop
we can't make it slow
do you wanna go?

*End song.*

### Real World Moment 6

**Conrad** (*selects an audience member to answer the below questions. The answers are used as the basis of a freestyle rap, performed by* **Jr**)

Who wants to move out eventually from where they live?
What's your name?
What job do you do?
Where do you live?
How much rent do you pay?
How many bedrooms do you have?
Who do you live with?
Are you happy with where you live?
Give me cheer if you think – will get their dream house!

**Conrad** (*selects a second audience member to answer the below questions. A second freestyle rap based on these answers is performed by* **Jr**)

Who has a dream home?
What's your name?
Where is the dream house?
How much does it cost?
What décor do you want on the walls?

**Real World Moment 7**

**Lakeisha**    At the back of my flats, we have a communal park. I remember as a kid going out the back to play amongst all that scattered litter on the tarmac flooring. You'd be lucky to find the slide without tidal wave like saliva in the middle, or swings that weren't decorated in chewing gum. I remember all that park litter being how my mate Stephen got me in trouble.

(*In the following* **Paul** *plays Stephen*).

'Oi Lakeisha! You see that white thing down by the swings, do you know what that's called?'

'No why what is it?'

'If I tell ya, pinky swear me you'll ask your mum when you go home.'

(*In the following* **Jr** *plays Lakeisha's mother with a Jamaican accent*).

'Mum?'

'Lakeisha. Ya na wash ya dutty hands after playing with ya friends and head straight to the fridge?'

'Oh yeah sorry, Mum. By the way Mum, what's a condom?'

'–WHAT?!' 'Where de hell did you hear that? Lakeisha. Who told you that dutty word?'

'Stephen mum. Stephen said it. Why what is it?'

'Never say that word again you hear – Stephen's very naughty for that, I don't like that Stephen. Him favour lizard — outta order. Imma tell his mumma!'

'Mum –'

'Na budda play wid Stephen from now on! Why don't you play wid Jordan, Leza and Danny? Na budda play with Stephen again. Or you can get out. Me say GET OUT! The only Stephen I wanna hear about is Steve Davis when him a'play snooker.'

So. Stephen was banned from my life outside of school.

By the way mum still hasn't told me what a condom is.

'Ah wa de bumbaclat...' (**Lakeisha** *cuts him off*)

But whether it was there to hide the odd needle or because a couple just had to have each other there and then – why would you bother to respect somewhere that isn't looked after in the first place anyway?

I look at all the nicer communal parks in areas outside of Lewisham borough and see people walking dogs, kids and families playing – just generally engaging with their parks in the way I suppose it's intended for them to.

I remember looking out the window at mine and seeing road men having communal meetings. I remember someone got shot.

I just wanted a clean space to play in with a bin at the side that was emptied every now and then.

And by the way Jr, my mum is Grenadian.

**Seems Like They've Won** (*musical number*)

**Luke** (*sung*)

> It seems like they've won.
> Because the madness has begun
> Let's have some fun . . .
> We swallowed their lies
> And we've eaten all the flies
> Perhaps we'll die!

(*Rapped*)

> Sold us a dream
> Must be a clown
> Cold cos the only thing that
> trickles down is blood
> Who's got the power now?
> Who's to blame?
> I remember staring at the TV at the
> tower
> All of the flames
> Nobody knows those people's names
> This is just a game
> The Third Way
> I'm screaming down the corridor
> Nobody heard me
> Nobody heard us
> Why they wanna hurt us?
> They turning they back
> They're alright jack
> I'm pulling down my cap
> What's the point?

Nobody's annoyed
Everybody's getting boyed
By Lord Fauntleroy
Why they arse-kissing you?
Should be dissing you
Why we not pissed with your lies?
Open up your mouth
And eat the flies.

**Luke** (*sung*)

It seems like they've won
Because the madness has begun
Let's have some fun
We swallowed their lies
And we've eaten all the flies,
Perhaps we'll die!

**Tony** (*rapped*)

Once virtuous, now standing on the
verges, trying to test who can fall
the furthest. There's been surges
in the circuits, the animals have
been let loose and taken over the
circus. Dogs in the burgers, blood
in the pools, shut down the centres
and shut down the schools. Climbing
the walls, carrying tools, hunting
in packs like blood-thirsty wolves.
They want resources, they want
power, they want a saviour, cometh
the hour, they will devour the
tower and then cower when it all
comes crumbling down in a shower
yet above it all, on a pedestal,
watching it all untouchable, and
unreachable, unseen like a dream
unspeakable, lies the true power on
top of this cathedral.

**Luke**

It seems like they've won
Cos the madness has begun

Let's have some fun
We swallowed their lies
And we've eaten all the flies
Perhaps we'll die!

**Luke** (*cont'd*)

It seems like they've won
Cos the madness has begun
Let's have some fun.

*End song.*

## Real World Moment 8

**Conrad**    When I was young, me and my brother Barry used to dream about leaving the estate. Just running away together.

'Bro – One day I'm gonna leave this shit hole.'

(**Lakeisha** *plays Conrad's brother.*)

'Yeah? How?'

'I dunno. Be famous innit? Be a table tennis champ, be a singer. Do shows, buy a house me and you can live in.'

'But what about wifeys and that?'

'They can move in with us, if we decide that we want to have wives then yeah.'

'So what you telling me now? How long you reckon we're gonna live together then?'

'Dunno, forever maybe. Yeah?'

**Jr** (*interrupting*)    Hold on, how old were you when you and Barry had this conversation?

**Conrad**    Dunno . . . . fifteen

**Jr**    Fifteen? You thought you were going you live forever with your brother at fifteen?

**Conrad**    Yeah . . . I dunno. We used to go on these long walks along the river Wandle. We wanted to get lost. But we returned home when it was dark and when we were hungry. Not that there was food waiting for us – we cooked for ourselves ever since we were like eleven.

**Jr**   I just can't believe that you thought that you were going to live forever with your brother when you were fifteen!

**Conrad**   Yeah . . . Never happened though.

**Jr**   Why?

**Conrad**   He got a girlfriend. Prick. We were supposed to leave together. He lives on another estate now . . . So it's like he never left. He said that he would never end up living on an estate . . .

**Jr**   That's pretty errr normal though right? He got a girlfriend?

**Conrad**   Yeah. He hates it there. But I guess he's lucky really.

### Announcement

**Tony** (*Spoken, line breaks indicate a slight musicality/rhythm to the language.*)

This is a facilities services'
announcement.
City Heights Primary on the twenty-third
floor has been closed due to arson.
The culprits remain at large.
The middle floor swimming
facilities will
be closed until further notice due
to the mutilated remains of Mark One
resident, Ms Carla Jones,
found floating, on Monday afternoon
at three pm.
Floors one, two and three have
now officially been declared a no
go area unless armed. Middle and
upper floor residents are to
activate their weapon entitlement
and are to report to their nearest
armory. Homicide, rape and pillage
of floors three and below is now
officially sanctioned.
And now to the main news. I am
delighted to inform you that
floor thirty-four resident, Bradley St Valentine's

first batch of craft beer,
Rustic Testicle
is now exclusively
available in the thirty-third floor
Nicholas Cohen memorial bar. The
beer is a fruit, spice, chocolate
and fish infused lager, picked with
the finest hops and brewed to
perfection.
Congratulations to Rosie Lucian-De
Grass, who recently qualified for
the second round of the
annual City Heights roof-top
Equestrian championship.
And finally, Dr David Smith is no
longer seeing patients in the
middle floor surgery, and will only
be accepting private clients,
payments must be made in Pure
Bolivian cocaine.

**David and Tony Part 3** (*rapped over instrumental*)

**David**

Tony, Fetch me a glass of Martini,

*Wait four beats.*

**David** (*cont'd*)

Tony, tell me a joke, humour me.

*Wait four beats.*

**David** (*cont'd*)

Tony turn the heating down half a
Degree.

*Wait four beats.*

**David** (*cont'd*)

Tony, it's far too chilly.

*Wait four beats.*

**David** (*cont'd*)

Tony, feed me, I need feeding!

**Doctor**

Tony, clean me, I need cleaning!

**David**

Tony, I'd like some female company!

**David** (*cont'd*)

Tony, four Mark One young lassies!

**David** (*cont'd*)

Tony, fuck them all right for me!
Tony, faster, they adore me!
Tony, harder, I'm so horny!
Tony, faster, I want glory!
Tony, take me to the top floor!

*Cut music.*

Tony, don't ignore me!
Tony, Take me, the top floor, now, Tony,
Tony, nowwwwwww . . .

**Sand Castles** (*musical number*)

**Luke**

It's been a while, but I still
think about you
How it all went down
How I acted like a damn fool
I regret it, I hope one day
you will forget it
You've got the things
That you said you would
You look happy
And I guess that's good
You said it,
I always believed that you'd get it
We live many lifetimes in our lives
You were one of the best . . .

Buildings don't let people down
People let the buildings down
Shiny towers we can't reach
Sand castles on the beach.

Buildings don't let people down
People let the buildings down
Shiny towers we can't reach
Sand castles on the beach.

(*Rapped*)

Monstrous monuments
Dehumanise occupants
residing at the top,
grotesque opulence,
it's obvious that, this evil edifice
makes it seem like they're scared of us
picture this perverse property
produce self-fulfilling prophecy
we don't grow properly in restricted
residences
can't you see, awful abodes,
I got dreams of different area codes
that I'll never see
I just wanna be
but Frankenstein flats create hate,
they're in hell surrounded by gates
and we forever wait,
and we forever wait

(*sung*)
Buildings don't let people down
People let the buildings down
Shiny towers we can't reach
Sand castles on the beach
Buildings don't let people down
People let the buildings down
Shiny towers we can't reach
Sand castles on the beach.

*End song.*

**Tough at the Top Remix** (*musical number, rapped*)

**Tony**

Mr Luke I'm here to inform you,

you have twenty-four hours to vacate the
premises.

**Luke**

What the hell is this?
Where am I gonna go?

**Tony**

Not my business
should have thought of this
before you moved into a double flat.

**Luke**

She's moved upstairs,
how could I control that?

**Tony**

It was prewritten into your tenancy
contract.

**Luke**

Where am I gonna go then?

**Tony**

Twenty-four hours.

**Luke**

Where am I gonna go then?

**Tony**

It's out of my power.

**Luke**

Where the fuck am I gonna go?

**Tony**

Mr Luke, I don't know.
You have twenty-four hours to vacate,
I do hope you've enjoyed your stay.

**Luke**

Fucking great.
I guess hard work pays.

**Michelle**

Dave babe can you pass me a drink?

**David**

I used to think
I was smarter
Could see further.

**Michelle**

Dave is this even worth it?

**David**

I used to use my telescope
Filled me with hope
Hour after hours looking up
to the top of the towers
I knew I was gonna be there.

**Michelle**

Dave do you even care?

**David**

I used to laugh at the kids
With the plastic kaleidoscopes
Looking through my lens
Thanking God, I was never them.

**Michelle**

Dave, you haven't fucked me in weeks,
All you seem to do is sleep
Now you're weak with the D
Are you looking at me?
I spoke to Tony
And he told me
That you wanted him to do me
Do me!
Do me?
Do me?

I must be fucking stupid!

**David**

>It's not natural to see that far
>To reach that far
>Could have used my own eyes to see
>The stars' stars
>The fucked up thing
>The kids with the kaleidoscope
>Really saw reality
>Even with their eyes closed
>But
>Look mum I made it!
>Your grown son
>Gave me the strength to believe
>It could be done.

**Luke**

>It's tough at the top
>Do you wanna go?
>It moves so fast
>It won't stop
>You can't make it slow
>Do you wanna go?

*End song.*


**Final Announcement**

**Tony** (*Spoken, line breaks indicate a slight musicality/rhythm to the language.*)

>This is a facilities services'
>announcement. Occupant, Mark One, Mr
>Luke has been formally evicted from
>City Heights, whilst being escorted
>from the premises he violently
>assaulted Nigel, Mark One security,
>who now has a minor graze on his
>forearm. If Mr Luke returns to the
>premises, kill him.
>Occupant, Dr David, Floor twenty-four. His

screams as he passed each floor on
the way down resembled the sound of
a child singing into a fan. He took
two point three seconds to hit the ground, a
new record. Facilities are
attending to the clean-up.
Occupant, Miss Michelle, Floor twenty-four,
She's still there, sat on the
floor, eating a bag of chips.
She made it.
Hard work pays off.


**Real World Moment 9**

**Paul**   So, when we were making this show, Conrad thought it would be
a good idea if we each used our own, real life stories.

**Jr**   So we gave him our real life stories but then we realised that
Conrad hadn't told us his, so we asked him, Conrad, where's your real
life story?

But then we wished we hadn't asked him . . .

*Move into*

**Fucking in the Room Next Door** (*musical number*)

**Conrad** (*sung*)

Turn out the lights, let's do it
tight, turn *Judge Judy* off . . . .
Ooh let's get lost
Pull back the sheets, keep on your
Socks, cos I'm a freak, don't
make the bed creak,
Fucking with your mum next door,
girl don't make a sound,
Fucking with your mum next door,
stay in that position
Fucking with your mum next door
Please don't make a sound
I just heard someone at the door,
Let's try again tomorrow!

*End song.*

**Real World Moment 10**

**Conrad**    I never have left Mitcham. I moved out with my mum into a
council house, on a street. I wanna move out, but I don't want to rent
privately. I'm waiting to move up a list.

I hate the idea that some rich landlord will be getting my hard earned
gold coins. And even after all those years of scheming with Barry to
leave Mitcham, now I don't want to leave. It's my community. I know
who to say 'hello' to ('You good yeah?'), who to chat shit to, and who to
avoid. The best cafes and the best times to go to the gym. I was there
when McDonald's closed down and all the crackheads came. We waited
thirty years for the train station! Now there's loads of new people . . .

M town. I had my first kiss there. Wrote my first song, and got arrested
for the first (and hopefully last time) there. I go to the housing office and
ask they have any places, they say, 'No, not even in Croydon'. What the
fuck?! The Whitgift Centre is not even popping anymore.

They did recommended some bedsits and one place that actually had
blood up the walls. I tell my mum, who wants me out, that there aren't
any places available yet. And she yells, 'What!? Not even in Croydon?'

Didn't think I was allowed there, Mum.

I walk through one of my old estates every day to go to Morrisons.

I look up to the top of one of my old blocks, at all of the floors, the front
doors exactly the same, just at different states of disrepair. Wondering if I
will get my own place up there. Sometimes it's like I'm actually still
there. I haven't actually left.

I'm just in post-estate mode.

**What Floor? Remix** (*musical number*)

**Conrad** (*sung*)

> What floor are we on?
> How do we get off?
> And does God know
> that we're here?

**Conrad** (*rapped*)

> Think of the city I see a list of
> things unjust, so much gold, right
> next to the rust, and through my
> fitted cap, I can see a map of
> inequality and austerity right next
> to prosperity, see the way power
> changes people and people's lives,
> truth becomes lies, open up your
> London eyes, so much rhetoric
> coming from their mouths, we should
> refuse to listen, leave it to the
> scientists and the politicians, is
> it graceful to lose if something
> hateful wins? We're dimming the
> suns, just to save our skins.
> Keep looking up.

**Conrad** (*sung*)

> What floor are we on?
> How do we get off and does God know
> that we're here?
> What floor are we on?
> How do we get off?
> And does God know
> that we're here?

*End.*

# Reflections: An Interview with Beats & Elements

*In June 2021, Beats & Elements company members met with the editor of this volume at Battersea Arts Centre (BAC) to discuss their processes and the significance of publishing these plays. The below is a text of that discussion, edited and abridged from a recording. These reflections offer a wider context for this anthology, which might feed into and enrich your understanding and interpretation of the plays.*

## On Process

**Conrad**   Go on Lakeisha, you start – because you work with two very different ways of writing. Collaboration is the main way that I work. But you also, you sit down and write scripts, and then you work in this collaborative way with us as well.

**Lakeisha**   Normally when I write a script, it's quite a solitary thing. You maybe get feedback on it when you've had loads of time to stare at it, and redraft it. You are creating a world out of one mind. And then everyone has to try and envision it and bring it to life. But the way that we work as a company is there's a starting idea, and the idea might be discussed, maybe we come up with a story and a through-line and stuff – and Conrad might create some music based on what we've talked about. And then individually in the same room we will write together. We would come up with a brief, like maybe about a specific character, and write in the rehearsal space. Then someone might say, 'Do you want to listen to this? I'm ready to share back.' The great thing is you get to hear someone else's part of this puzzle, and then you share your part, and you get that instant feedback and that instant response.

**Conrad**   Yeah and when anyone hears Lakeisha's verses they're like: 'That's it I'm changing my verse now! I'm changing my verse!'

*Everyone laughs.*

**Lakeisha**   There's a lot of trial and error. There've been times when I've tried something and realised it's not ready. And then sometimes what comes to you, you feel more connected to it and like, 'Yeah, this feels right'. And then sometimes when someone else shares their stuff, it gives you a perspective you maybe didn't have, and informs what you're writing. So, it's super, super collaborative, even if you're just individually writing a few lines, because you're sharing back straight away to people that are writing to the same musical tapestry.

**Paul**    There were slightly more structured writing exercises, where like Lakeisha mentions there would be a provocation to a piece of music. And there'd also be an element of maybe us jamming with an idea, performing to each other, improvising, and something else would come out of that – quite often it was a chorus, or I'm probably right in saying, at least one or two whole new pieces of music. It's sort of quite a loose structure that we had, that allowed room for us to improvise. And with both *Foxes* and *High Rise* we found initial stimulus in books. So, we'd talk ideas through from those. With *Foxes* we had both read the *Chavs*[1] book, and had lots of discussions about class. And then for *High Rise*, Con had read *High-Rise*[2] I think, and so we all went away and read that.

**Conrad**    I felt that we could improve it to be honest. I felt that *High-Rise* was a good book, but we could make it a lot better. This is a good concept, but he hasn't done it right. He didn't finish it off. And I felt like we improved it. Obviously it's our own ideas – it's not an official retelling of the original. But we kept an allusion to the original book. There's no point in covering up your sources because it's hip hop theatre, right? Sampling is part of it.

**Lakeisha**    Sampling the book. I think that's an amazing term.

**Jr**    Sampling the book . . . I never heard that phrase before! The thing is, in terms of the writing, I'm not a writer, but once I'm given a script from Paul or Con, because we know each other very well, they can be like, 'This will suit you'. So, I know it's never going to be too far-fetched for me to perform. But at the same time, it's a stretch. Because you have to bring an energy to it that's believable. I remember one time we were in rehearsal and Paul and Con gave me a note of how to come across when we were doing the David and Tony scene. And I remember, because of the upper-class position David's in, I remember doing that scene in a well-spoken way the first time you see Tony and David – and then halfway through the rehearsals Con said, 'You should play it like this, less upper-class.' And it felt right. So that was really interesting and fun. In terms of writing lyrics, like Lakeisha was saying, it was about going off ideas, working with everyone else. I try not to listen to anyone else, especially Lakeisha cos she's like, golden with the pen.

**Paul**    In our collaborative process, I think it's worth mentioning, you're catching a vibe. Because there were days when not everyone could make it, and if there's a certain vibe on that day – like Con makes a loop and we jam around it – we might create something for someone who isn't there that comes out of a particular vibe, and that person would then take those verses and make it their own. It's a certain amount of putting your faith in the ether, in whoever is in the room that day, and trusting the energy in the room and running with it. There's certain verses in the show that might have been started by one person, rapped by someone else, someone else adds something in – all this cross-writing and this process of layering from being in a room and vibing.

**Conrad**    Yes. It's about the process of who is there. It's fine if people have off days, are more quiet sometimes, are late or need to leave. The idea of professionalism meaning you have to be on time and on form every day, that's some bullshit passed down – a lot of people are misguided by drama schools and other theatre people about what being professional is actually about. There is such a thing as discipline, but you need to find out what works for you. And that's about being authentic. How the hell are you gonna be a great artist if you can't listen to your own body and to the rhythms in the room? Read a room or you're gonna be shit. You're wasting energy. Maybe you need to sit down over here quietly in the corner, or maybe you need to rant today – that feeds into the work. Whereas the whole 'leave your problems at the door' – that's why we've got whack shows with no life in them! Leave it at the door? No, bring it in. Bring it in. I don't understand if you're making art how you leave it at the door. What's in here then? What's inside?

## On Class

**Conrad**    Class is very important for us. I think hip hop and rap are intertwined with class. It's about class struggle around the world. That's why people try to denigrate hip hop, try to capitalise on it – so it can be discredited. So it can become a saleable commodity. But actually, it's about working-class stories. And hip hop histories are rooted in frustration and struggle. I guess I'm interested in rappers that are from those backgrounds. I'm not interested in posh kids rapping. I'm interested in hearing the struggle. In the voice you can hear when there's some pain, when there's some bullshit there. Maybe some of the working-class rappers don't have as many words in their lexicon, but you don't need that. You need the pain of struggle. I think class is very important because that's about acknowledging where this form has come from. It is also to do with understanding why there's slang, why things are said in certain ways. And that's about not changing things for a middle-class audience, but presenting what you want to do on stage and fuck everyone else.

**Paul**    I come from, probably you'd say a lower middle-class background. I left home at twenty and had to work, didn't have any money, blah blah blah. I just did the usual, just trying to earn a living. But I think with the class aspect of it, when I met Con and the rest of these guys, I felt like I could talk to these three and they would understand me more than if I talked to a lot of the other people in theatre buildings – we had a lot more in common, and I think that's related to the language similarities, similar experiences – not the same – but a lot of similarities. And I guess, cultural taste, maybe? There's certain things I can say to these guys that I won't be able to say to anyone else who works in the theatre.

**Lakeisha**    I think people can become really distracted. If you're having a conversation with someone they can become really distracted by the fact that they're projecting a lot of stuff onto you, because maybe there's consonants that I don't pronounce. Or because I'm wearing a hat or wearing a hoodie or whatever. And you can decide in your head how intelligent I am, how intelligent I look. And it doesn't even matter what I'm saying because they are so distracted by the accent, or because where they grew up they never saw anyone like me or heard anyone like me – they only saw people who fall into those categories in certain roles on television shows, or films or whatever it was. So, it's nice to be able to work with artists where you are not having those projections put on you. You are talking to each other as humans, like you would your friends or your family.

**Conrad**    We're working together, but it's not exhausting. Because I'm not having to . . .

**Lakeisha**    . . . Prove you're intelligent, or you might have something valuable to say or whatever it is.

**Conrad**    We can just chat. I don't feel like I've got to think this, do that.

**Lakeisha**    With us, you're judged when someone gets to know you well enough to work out if you have bad morals or you're not that intelligent, as opposed to them thinking they know that about you already because they've seen you and heard you speak a sentence. For me personally on my journey, I know that I've been in rooms where – I've not necessarily spoken RP[3] in those rooms and turned myself into something I'm not – but, I have adapted. There's a lot of adapting that needs to be done in the theatre industry, with different groups of people. One thing I really like about Conrad, not that I've been in every space he has ever been in his life, but whenever I've seen him he is consistently the same in every circumstance. I'm like, how does he do that!?

**Conrad**    I think it would be great if everyone could be like that. I feel like the space we create, we're creating a model for other people. It would be great if others could do the same thing. We should be allowed to be ourselves, innit? If I'm thinking about this and that and that I'm limiting what I say, I'm limiting my own creativity.

**Jr**    I'm definitely working class. When I went to drama school, before the first day I was like, 'I can't wear a cap, can I? Can I be me?' In the end I was like, 'Ok, I'll be me', and I just went there being me.

**Conrad**    But if you even have to process the thought of, 'What am I gonna do?' that's a little bit of energy you've had to waste. Whereas other people they get to be themselves all day.

**Jr**    A hundred per cent!

**Paul**    On this, one of the things I really value about working the way we do is that you can be yourself. I started doing theatre workshops, getting involved in theatre programmes, when I was about twenty-five. It was all quite new to me, and quite often in theatre workshops there would be an element of almost spirituality. So at the start, it would be, 'Ok we're gonna just do some mindfulness work, deep breathing'. Sometimes you do these all-day workshops where, 'We're gonna sit down together, we're gonna prepare food together'. All of this stuff, for me, it was really alien. But I thought, 'Oh, maybe this is how it is. This is what you've got to do. Maybe I've got to do this then.' But when we started working together, Con was like, 'You ain't gotta do that'. He said, 'Someone's decided that's the way of doing things and everyone's just gone along with it. But if that's not you, then that's not part of you, so don't do it.' And I felt relieved. I haven't got to sit through this feeling really awkward, pretending I know what's going on. Whereas actually, we be ourselves and find our own ways of working. You haven't got to take part in this sort of performative ritual, that maybe some people are really into. And that's fine. But not everyone.

**Conrad**    And you *don't* have to do those things. Maybe some people won't prevail if you do all that touchy shit, touching each other, rolling round on the floor. It's off-putting. A lot of people feel they maybe have to do that – but not everybody has that experience of cuddling and touching strangers, or their parents even. That way of working can alienate certain people.

**Jr**    I think it's so important to feel seen. To go to the theatre and see shows that you come out and think, 'Yeah I resonate with that'. You can see a show and come out and be like, 'Oh the show's good', 'Great acting, good storyline'. But when you watch something like *No Milk for the Foxes* – that just really resonated with me. Obviously with the class system it was the first time I watched something and was like, 'This is spot on. I know people like that, I've worked with people like that. They're in my environment.' A lot of feedback I got from friends who came to watch *High Rise* – and they don't go to the theatre, they're not part of the theatre world, and if they do it's the big shows in the West End and it's a big day out – but when they come to see *High Rise* and it's us guys singing and rapping, the black hoodies and the hats, they're like: 'What have I been missing out on?' And yeah. This is theatre.

## On Hip Hop

**Conrad**    I think our shared love of music and hip hop helps our process. Like when I first met you, Lakeisha, I still remember you told me to listen to a Kendrick Lamar mixtape. That was the very first thing you said, so I knew straight away. And I never became a Kendrick Lamar fan, but you knew music and you were recommending rappers. And I guess it's the same with all of us, innit? We realise how rap can change a text – now we're rapping a speech it has a different feeling. Different allusions with the rhythm and cadence. It feels more authentic actually.

**Paul**    I guess with me, my background in performing is emceeing. So, drum and bass and garage and all of that. But hip hop I listened to since I was a kid. When I started emceeing seriously, with drum and bass, I would rap at half the speed. I was essentially rapping at hip hop tempos, and I started making hip hop and it went from there. When I started making theatre, I came to BAC. I came here, and for me theatre was very much a separate thing. I was almost a bit embarrassed about the hip hop. But when I did my first show here, I found out in the building was Conrad and he runs the Beatbox Academy and he has his own hip hop theatre company. For me that concept of hip hop being in theatre, I had this quite narrow minded idea of what theatre was – I didn't know anything honestly. And then I met Con and we worked on a show together and it was like, 'Yeah! I can do hip hop in theatre!' And at the end of the day, it's not about doing hip hop theatre for the sake of it, but he said, 'You rap don't you? That's your skillset. So why would you not do it in theatre? If that's something you can already do. And that's how you express yourself? Of course you take that in there.' And I'm twenty-five by the time I start doing theatre, I've got bad diction, I've not been to drama school as a kid, I'm not gonna be an RSC actor am I? But what I've already got is a lexicon that I've worked on with rap.

**Conrad**   I remember when you said, 'I do spoken word.' And I said, 'Is that cos you're embarrassed to rap?' I remember saying that to you. 'Is it cos you haven't got the balls to rap?' Because it seems like everyone that did spoken word really wanted to rap, but in the theatre it had more credibility to call it 'spoken word' . . .

**Paul**   Yeah, yeah there was definitely an element of that. Not for me personally, for me it was fun. I started rapping, but writing stuff without a beat was fun to me. Spoken word was just another medium, but there were definitely people like that. People who did rap but they wanted to seem like they're involved in a more serious artform, so they call it 'spoken word'.

**Conrad**   But that's a piss-take, innit? Because it's like shitting on a whole other artform.

**Paul**   Completely. Yeah. But for me doing hip hop theatre was a leap of faith. And coming to it with someone who was already steeped in it. I dunno how many shows your company[4] had done, like three or four?

**Conrad**   Yeah. Well, we did one big show[5] and a few others.

**Paul**   I remember giving you my mixtape – and we worked on a show together and Con was like, 'Come to my studio and we'll make some music'. And eventually it was like, 'Oh, do you want to make a show?' And I'm a rookie in this, I'm totally green. Here's someone that's already in the game and had had a company and had reviews and done shows and shit – and he wants to work with me? But I think partly it's because of the hip hop thing. He knew I rapped and there probably weren't many people in this building that did. And so, you know . . . .

**Conrad**   It's funny, a producer here, Liz, was like, 'You gotta meet Paul, you gotta meet Paul'. And I thought, 'Who's this dickhead?' So that's how we started working together. With Jr, we met at college and have been working together for years.

**Jr**   Yeah. The journey's long. At South Thames College I met Con. He was playing his guitar, looked like Elvis. Everyone was like, 'You look like Elvis man, you look like Elvis'. And because it was the Elvis look, it wasn't cool. But I was like, 'No no, this guy, he's on the music thing. He's always on the guitar, he's always asking questions. I need to be with this guy. This guy's got something'. I remember he had his guitar, and he was strumming away like he does, and I was like, 'Can I freestyle on it?' And he was like, 'Yeah, cool'. And then he's like, 'You gotta come to my house'. I went to his house to record some music. So anyway, fast-forward, we're doing shows. My first ever show was in an elderly home. All old people. Me and Con would just be there, baggy jeans, doo-rag, Nike top, pair of Tims. Really thought I was a hip hop star. These old people appreciated it – it was great.

**Conrad**    No, they really did, innit?

**Jr**    They did appreciate it.

**Conrad**    Whenever we went and did rapping and stuff the OAPs, maybe it was because they didn't get to see much, but they really loved it. We rapped to someone who was a hundred years old, do you remember?

**Jr**    Yeah! The thing with me was I was a fiend. I just wanted to rap. If there's a beat let me jump on it. We'd go to karaoke, and there's songs on the screen, obviously, but I'm just trying to rap on the karaoke set. Con and Con's brother came up with their company, TdC, and we started making plays with rapping. That was the first time I was like, 'Right, so there isn't really a difference'. Because I wanted to be an actor, but I also wanted to rap – I didn't want to be a rap artist, I wanted to be an actor. I just loved rapping – but this was the first time they came together, and I was like, 'You can do this for a living?' I still can't believe I'm in this position, with a team who are as tight as me, if not better in ways. I'm always learning from these guys. It keeps me challenged. Because I think if you're just like, 'I'm there I've done it, cool', then your journey doesn't continue. And as you get older as well, my friend said it the other day actually, a friend from my school group, 'What you gonna do Jr, be forty and be rapping still?' And I was like, 'Yeah. Probably yeah.'

**Paul**    There's this idea, particularly with rap, that it's this thing you do where you're posing around like a young kid. But does an impressionist painter who does it in their twenties, are they asked, 'Why you still doing that in your forties?' It lacks that analysis that other art forms get. Writing verses and performing those verses, that's a craft right?

**Jr**    But they see it as a young man's sport. So, if you're not young and you're still doing it, you're looked down on.

**Conrad**    But that's to discredit it.

**Jr**   Of course, but that's how they see it. But at the end of the day as Paul was saying, it's an artform and if you're very good at what you're doing people will enjoy it. People enjoy music for all different reasons.

**Lakeisha**   I love hip hop, but as a performer, I don't mind – if I'm going to work with a theatre company in the cast – I don't mind working with the practices of that company. Whatever they feel we need to become an ensemble, as long as it's not something that goes against my morals or whatever, I'm happy to crack on. But if I was working with a company and it was clear their gods were, you know, certain types of standard theatre practitioners, but they wanted rap in the show for some reason, I wouldn't give that to a group of people who didn't respect this artform, who felt like rap was just a trend, novelty add-on thing. Whereas when you're working with people who respect this artform, then it's different. The other aspect to that is this thing of when you come in a package that people make assumptions about, where you walk into spaces – and yes you choose to wear the clothes you want to wear, but it's what you wear – but when you walk into spaces and you feel like in those spaces people think you're a rapper, gatecrashing a theatre – as if that was a bad thing – but the last thing I need now is for those people to have me rapping in their show. Because then they'll go, 'Oh we'll never cast her in anything else, because she's everything we thought.' Because people are easily distracted by extra layers of stuff that they can't get past.

**Conrad**   I think the more we own this, the more power we have. Because other people can't do it, they try, but how long they been doing it for? One second? Fuck off. And I feel like something that was a weakness has become a strength.

**Paul**   I think for a lot of the audiences we've gone up in front of now, they are seeing something they can resonate with, like what Jr was talking about earlier. But anyone can watch our stuff. Essentially we've made a play, it's just that the form has rapping in it, and beatboxing. It takes a leap of faith – but once you get over that, there's a story, there's characters, there's things going on – like there is in any other play. I think when we made *Foxes*, the responses we got, most of them positive, along the lines of, 'I can't believe we're seeing something that represents us.' But also, there were negative responses – there were a couple of snarky little blogs. It was like, 'Oh we're doing the right thing then'. Because the person who wrote the snarky blog doesn't understand it. Therefore, they've got to go away and do some work now to understand what this form is – and not just the form, but the people that are being portrayed. Cos clearly they weren't getting it. I think that shows we're on the right path then.

## On Publishing

**Conrad**   We never imagined our work would get published, because of
the way we wrote it. We collectively put it together – I don't think we
imagined that that kind of work gets published. Also, because the fact is,
it's loads of rap, in a play. There are no gods in that, there's no canon.
The importance of this publication is it legitimises what we're doing.
Rap is literature and it is a valid theatre form. It's pretty important. I
hope other young artists will be inspired by it – they'll think, 'That's
great, maybe I could do it', or even if it's, 'I could do better than that',
that's all right. I wanted to be better than Ballard, but Ballard is still to
me a god, he is still amazing. We're all standing on the shoulders of
giants, wanting to be better.

**Lakeisha**   People publish for all sorts of reasons. The same reason
people want album lyrics, to decipher more about the words. Or they
want a play script so they can go away and read the play themselves,
learn about the characters, maybe even play the characters. At Samuel
French's back in the day,[6] you'd go there, and you'd try to find a
monologue for an audition – if I saw *High Rise* or *No Milk* there, I would
have been mind-blown. I remember just looking for Roy Williams.[7] Or
finding characters who weren't that great, or who were really great, who
I couldn't do justice to. It would have been like a dream come true if I
saw *High Rise* or *No Milk* or *DenMarked* on those shelves. It is like,
there's so much poetry and layers in a lot of the words, and the
storytelling as a whole. I think it deserves to be studied and read and
used for people to practice their love of acting – to hone their craft, their
love of writing, by looking at these plays. It's really important.

**Paul**   It allows for legacy doesn't it? Because making theatre can be
fleeting. You spend all this time and heart and energy making the show.
And you do the show – however long it is, one night or a tour, and then
it's over. It exists in people's memories and whatnot, but when you've
got the lyrics and the descriptors laid down in a book – it exists forever
now. And maybe it will go on to have another life with us, or maybe
some young students will fancy giving it a go. Or trying to . . . like we
did with *High-Rise* the book, take our play and reinterpret it and try and
make it better.

**Conrad**   One thing I just want to point out is we tell our own stories –
so Lakeisha from Blue Borough,[8] who's got a hardworking mum, who
tells stories about herself, is in print. I almost feel emotional thinking
about that. Those stories are in print, the real stories of our lives. That is
what I wanted to see in print. Maybe that sounds really conceited but the

stories I wanted to see, in the forms I wanted to see them, rap and story-telling exist now. Hip hop theatre, it isn't about rap, it's about where truth is being told and that's so important. I talk about my council estate. Hearing the word 'estate', reading it in a script that was written by working-class people, ethnic minorities, that's important. It would have meant a lot for me at fourteen, twelve, to have read that. And if any young students read it now, they won't know the extent of what it means and that's good. It will be normal to them to read plays they can relate to. I always found reading plays empty because it was like, 'I don't relate to the character, I don't relate to the story, nothing about this relates to my life. And ok, I'll believe it's real, but I'm making a logical leap to say this character seems real. I don't know anyone like that. I don't know anything that's happened like that. I don't know any families like that!' None of these stories were real to me.

**Lakeisha**    I remember teachers at BRIT School[9] would say, 'Do you see how Dunyasha in *The Cherry Orchard* is kind of like you and me . . . ?' and it's like, 'No'.

**Conrad**    NO! It's a horrible feeling.

**Jr**    Yeah it's amazing to be honest. I can die and know I'm part of history in the genre I love. Acting and music. In my mind whenever I see a post about the anthology being published, I just see myself walking into the library at my drama school and thinking, 'None of these books connect with me'. I'm forcing it because I'm here, I'm forcing to be like everyone else . . . . but really that's not me. I can appreciate the writing and storyline but that's not me. So, to read our stories – Paul's segment when he talks about seventeen addresses, that done something to me. Seventeen addresses, and I ain't even left home.

**Paul**    It's nineteen now.

**Jr**    Nineteen addresses! Woah. He's doing everything to keep up with his dream, and I'm living at home trying to keep up with my dream. And he can see my journey, I can see his, and they're different, but you can respect each other.

**Paul**    You know a genuinely pleasant moment for me was – we talk about the collaborative nature of what this is, but when I saw the publishing agreement, not just seeing my name on there but these three. All our names together on the agreement. All with parity. And I felt happy that my name was there, but my friends are on there too. And they are all to me highly skilled, excellent executioners in what they do. Seeing my friends doing well . . . the fact that my name's on there is a bonus. It's like you are winning times three or four. And it hadn't set in until I got that email and see all our names on it.

**Lakeisha**    What's crazy I've realised as well about those real life stories – sometimes people look at fictional books, novels and plays, to gain historical insights into particular periods of time. It's just so crazy that if people want to look into class issues, maybe in London specifically, or in the UK in the twenty-first century, this could be a reference point. These clues that we use to try to find out about the nineteenth century by picking up a book . . . . our reality is there now. That's not to say everyone had nineteen addresses, or lived with their mum until they were this age or whatever – but it's like, 'What does this tell you about the world at that time if this was the situation for those four people?' It's mind blowing that this could be a future reference point. It's crazy.

## Notes

1   Owen Jones, *Chavs: The Demonisation of the Working Class* (London: Verso 2011).
2   J. G. Ballard, *High-Rise* (London: Jonathan Cape 1975).
3   'Received Pronunciation' or 'RP' is a formal British accent, usually associated with middle- and upper-class, highly educated, or 'posh', speakers. Unlike other British accents it is not associated with a specific region.
4   That company was 'Theatre de Cunt' or TdC. You can read more about them in the book by Katie Beswick and Conrad Murray, *Making Hip Hop Theatre: Beatbox and Elements* (London: Bloomsbury Methuen 2022).
5   *Hitler Wrote 20 Pop Songs. . . Have You Heard Them?* Battersea Arts Centre (2006).
6   Samuel French was a theatre bookshop located on Fitzroy Street in London, selling theatre books, plays and offering advice on audition monologues. It closed in 2017, but has since been re-established at the Royal Court Theatre based in London's Sloane Square.
7   Roy Williams is a playwright known for writing plays about the Black British experience, particularly plays set in urban contexts, often with a young cast.
8   'Blue Borough' is a colloquial term for the London Borough of Lewisham, where Lakeisha Lynch-Stevens is based.
9   The BRIT School is a free to attend performing arts school in south London.

# Glossary

*This glossary gives simple definitions of terms used in the plays that might be unfamiliar to some readers. Many of the below terms/words appear in the plays as slang, and where that is the case the slang meaning is given below. Of course, as explained in the hip hop lyricism essay, words, particularly slang words, especially used in lyrical contexts, rely on multiple, intersecting definitions to create meaning and feeling. Therefore, this glossary should be understood as a partial account, intended to help readers unfamiliar with particular words or phrases to comprehend the play texts and understand the direct meaning in a specific context. There is obviously much more that might be said about the use of language in the plays in this anthology – please take the definitions here as only a starting-point in your analysis.*

**Ain't**   A colloquial contraction of either 'am not/are not/is not', or 'has not/have not'. Common in London accents including cockney and MLE.

**Al Pacino**   Film star whose movies include *Scarface*, also played ex-con Carlo Brigante in the film *Carlito's Way*.

**Alright**   Contraction of 'all right', can be used as a friendly greeting, to confirm assent or to indicate that something is satisfactory/pleasant. Or, if posed as a question, to ask for assent or whether something is satisfactory/or to check the other person's mood.

**Asda George**   George at ASDA is a clothing brand for the supermarket ASDA, which is known for its low prices and is often considered poor quality.

**Bait**   Obvious/blatant/clear (as in, to make obvious, or see clearly) — especially illegal, immoral, embarrassing or secretive behaviour and actions.

**Bang** (as in 'bang her')   To have sex.

**Bar** (as in 'bar of it')   Some/any/an amount.

**Bare**   Many/a lot, or very/excessively.

**Beef**   To indicate anger towards a person, or the existence of a feud/argument between people/groups.

**Bellyache**   Something annoyingly protracted or unpleasant.

**Blue Peter badge**   An award for a trivial task, after the badges given to participants in tasks on the long-running BBC Children's show *Blue Peter*.

**BNP**   The British National Party, a far-right fascist political party.

**Bob Crow**    Charismatic leader who was the General Secretary of the National Union of Rail, Maritime and Transport Workers, died in 2014.

**Boyed**    To mock somebody, take advantage of them or take them for a fool.

**Bruv (or 'bro')**    Short for 'brother', a term of endearment for a friend, or indication that the speaker considers the person they are addressing as a friend/comrade.

**Buss**    To give (for free).

**Butlin's**    A family holiday seaside resort chain, with camps across the United Kingdom, popular with working-class people.

**Cake**    Money.

**Chav**    A derogatory term for a working class person, sometimes understood as an acronym for the phrase 'council housed and violent'.

**Cheddar**    Money.

**Chomp**    A chocolate-covered chewy caramel bar – in the 1990s each bar cost ten pence.

**Chopstix**    A chain of fast food restaurants serving Chinese-style cuisine.

**Cotchin'**    To rest or relax, or to sit/sleep somewhere for a short period of time.

**Croydon**    A town in south London, not glamorous.

**Cruyff turns**    A football move named after the Dutch international player Johan Cruyff.

**Cuss or cussing**    To insult.

**David Cameron**    Prime Minister of the UK between May 2010 and July 2016.

**DBS**    'Disclosure and Barring Service'; a DBS is a criminal record check carried out on employees or volunteers in the UK, usually those working in contexts with young or vulnerable people (especially in occupations such as nursing, teaching, childcare etc.).

**Double-decker bus**    A bus with two levels, famously the red coloured London buses are referred to as 'double-deckers'.

**Dough**    Money, especially bank notes.

**the Duke**    Nickname for the actor John Wayne.

**E Tablets (or 'Es')**    Ecstasy, an illegal drug, the tablet form of the chemical powder MDMA.

**Ends**    Locality or neighbourhood where you feel at home/where you are from or where your home is located.

**FarmVille**    An interactive game, connected to the social media platform Facebook, in which players undertook virtual agricultural management/farming work such as growing and harvesting crops.

**Freddo**    A frog shaped chocolate bar – known for costing ten pence in the 1990s.

**Fruities**    Fruit machines for gambling.

**a Grand**    One thousand pounds.

**Grassing**    Giving someone up to the authorities, reporting someone to the police. Derogatory term for doing this.

**Happy Shopper**    A very inexpensive brand of household products, popular with working-class people.

**Haven**    A chain of family holiday parks, located across the UK.

**Help the Aged**    A charity that supports the needs of older people.

**He-Man**    A fictional animated superhero.

**Illuminati**    A conspiracy in which a group of select unelected people from the power-elite control the world.

**Individual Education Plans or IEPs**    A document that assists teachers in planning for the teaching needs of individual students.

**Innit**    A contraction of the phrase 'isn't it'. Used to ask for or confirm agreement with a statement or question.

**Jacked**    Stolen.

**Jars** (as in 'a couple of jars')    An alcoholic drink, usually a pint of beer or lager.

**Jobsworth**    Someone who takes their job extremely seriously to the point of being annoying.

**John Wayne**    An American actor known for leading roles in Western and war films.

**JSA**    Jobseeker's Allowance, a form of welfare benefit for unemployed people who are looking for employment.

**Kip**    To sleep or nap.

**Kwik Save No Frills**    'No Frills' was an extremely inexpensive and unglamourous brand of household and food products sold by the budget supermarket Kwik Save.

**Lambeth Walk**    A popular song from the 1937 musical *Me and My Girl*, named after a street in London.

**Lord Fauntleroy**    A pompous or pampered member of the elite, usually considered undeserving of their position. Named after the eponymous character in Frances Hodgson Burnett's novel *Little Lord Fauntleroy*.

**'Low that**    Allow that – suggesting the person being addressed should let something happen without causing a fuss, should stop making a fuss, or should stop an annoying or persistent behaviour.

**Maccy D's**    The fast food chain McDonald's.

**Maglite**    A brand of high-quality, high-performance torches, often used by security services.

**Man dem**    Those people, that group of people (usually men or boys) – especially a group of friends.

**Masons**    Freemasons – members of an elite group with complex secret rituals established to provide mutual support and often considered to wield concealed political power.

**Mitcham (or 'M-Town')**    A district in the London Borough of Merton.

**Mug**    An idiot, fool or stupid person, also a cup for drinking.

**New Deal**    A workfare programme introduced by the New Labour government, which required unemployed people to undertake training and voluntary work in order to continue accessing unemployment benefits.

**New Era cap**    A brand of baseball caps, popular with UK rappers.

**Nicholas Cohen**    A British journalist, alive at the time of writing.

**Nicks**    A very cheap brand of trainers. The verb 'to nick' (nicked, nicks, nicking etc.) can also mean 'to steal, or take unlawfully'.

**Off-key**    Suspicious/not right.

**One armed bandits**    Fruit machines for gambling with a single handle or 'arm' at the side which is pulled to play.

**One man up**    Alone/solo.

**P's (or 'paper')**    Money.

**Page three**    A regular feature in the UK's *The Sun* newspaper where a photograph of a topless female model, usually with very large breasts, would appear on the third page.

**Paki bashing**    To attack/beat up those of south Asian or Pakistani descent.

**Panda Pop**    A brand of inexpensive soda, popular with school children.

**Paul Gascoigne**    An extremely famous English footballer.

**Pingit app**    A mobile phone app used for transferring money.

**Popping**    Exciting or with an upbeat and happy atmosphere.

**Preeing**    To observe or stare at something, particularly online or on social media.

**Road men**    Men or boys of questionable morals, who conduct their (usually illegal) activities in the street. Or those who are presumed to have questionable morals/be criminals due to their dress and presentation.

**Routemaster**    A style of front-engined double-decker London bus with an open platform at the back for boarding.

**Safe**    Indicates that something or someone is acceptable/pleasing.

**Shirker**    Someone who avoids work, this term has often been used by journalists and politicians to denigrate unemployment or welfare benefit recipients.

**Shot** (as in 'shot it')    Sold (particularly if the sale refers to illegal goods such as drugs or stolen items).